KENTISH

VII. KENT AND THE OXFORD MOVEMENT

Selected Documents

With a commentary by

NIGEL YATES, M.A., F.R. HIST. S.

ALAN SUTTON
FOR
KENT ARCHIVES OFFICE
1983

Other books in this series:

Kentish Sources: I.   *Some Roads and Bridges*

Kentish Sources: II.   *Kent and the Civil War*

Kentish Sources: III.   *Aspects of Agriculture and Industry*

Kentish Sources: IV.   *The Poor*

Kentish Sources: V   *Some Kentish Houses*

Kentish Sources: VI.   *Crime and Punishment*

(Kentish Sources volumes I to VI available only from Kent Archives Office).

Published by Alan Sutton Publishing Limited,
17a Brunswick Road, Gloucester GL1 1HG,
in collaboration with
Kent Archives Office.

ISBN 0 86299 064 5

Produced by Alan Sutton Publishing Limited
Printed in Great Britain by
Redwood Burn Ltd., Trowbridge, Wiltshire

TABLE OF CONTENTS

ILLUSTRATIONS

EDITORIAL NOTE

The publication of this volume marks the relaunching of the *Kentish Sources* series after an interval of some thirteen years, and the beginnings of a new policy of linking archival publications with archival exhibitions. The exhibition with which the publication of this volume is linked will be staged at the cathedrals of Canterbury and Rochester, and at churches in Folkestone, Maidstone, Ramsgate, Sevenoaks and Tunbridge Wells between April and July 1983.

When the *Kentish Sources* series first appeared the volumes marked a major new development in records publication, which was widely copied at both a local and a national level. Thirteen years later it is possible to build on this experience to make some significant changes in presentation although it is envisaged that there will be considerable flexibility in the presentation of future volumes in the series. In this present volume the principal differences from earlier volumes in the series has been the effective separation of the commentary from the documents, the publication of fewer but more substantial extracts from records, and the use of relevant documentary material outside the direct custody of the Kent Archives Office. One criticism of earlier volumes in the series was that they lacked indices; accordingly in the present volume simple indices of persons and places have been added.

The aim of this volume is to act as an introduction to the subject and to encourage future research by indicating the sources available and the sort of information they reveal. Whilst every attempt has been made in the commentary to link local and national events, it has not been possible to provide more than a fairly sketchy account of the national background. The primary aim of the footnotes, however, is to draw the reader's attention to the major works available that will give precisely that information, and that contain within them detailed guides to further reading. The present volume does not pretend to be a comprehensive or exhaustive study of the impact of the Oxford Movement in Kent. Such a volume would in any case tend, by the nature of the subject, to be rather repetitive and unreadable. There is, however, a good case for urging that individual case studies should be undertaken of particular communities or groups of communities in the county, since published work on the movement as it relates to Kent is negligible and the available sources, in diocesan, parish and private archives, are considerable.

Although I take full responsibility for the shortcomings of this volume, its compilation would have been impossible without the assistance of Maureen Shaw, Amanda Streeter and Kathleen Topping, who acted as research assistants, critics and chauffeurs, and of Ann Wale, who typed the whole volume from miscellaneous scraps of paper. I am also deeply indebted to the controlling bodies and professional staffs of the British Library, Lambeth Palace Library, Rochester Cathedral Library, Kent County Library (especially its Shepway division), the Council for the Care of Churches, and the individual churches cited in the main text, for access to and permission to reproduce documents or illustrations in their custody or ownership.

Nigel Yates

Feast of St. Wilfrid
12 October 1982

COMMENTARY

Introduction

Thirty years after the preaching of Keble's Assize Sermon on 14 July of that year, the future Cardinal Newman wrote 'I have ever considered and kept the day, as the start of the religious movement of 1833'.[1] The actual sermon, however, in which Keble accused the government of 'national apostasy' for suppressing a number of Irish bishoprics, was only one, by itself fairly insignificant, event in the launching of what has since been called the Oxford Movement, or the Catholic Revival in the Church of England.[2] It had been foreshadowed by the publication of Keble's volume of religious poems, *The Christian Year*, in 1827, and various meetings in Oxford and elsewhere of churchmen concerned about the condition of the established church. It was followed by a meeting at Hadleigh, which established an Association of Friends of the Church and engineered an address to the archbishop of Canterbury, and by the launching of the *Tracts for the Times*.

The 1820's and 1830's were ripe for some such movement as these events together brought about. The Church of England was at a crossroads and her more active members divided about which direction she ought to be travelling in. The crisis had been brought about by a mixture of contemporary events and trends: the seeming failure of the Church of England to cope with the demographic and social changes brought about by the industrial revolution; the political changes of the early nineteenth century which appeared to weaken the Anglican establishment and strengthen dissent; the fear of revolution; the romantic movement in architecture and literature; above all the feeling that Anglican leaders, especially the bishops, had abandoned the fight to preserve the independence and influence of the Church of England

[1] J.H. Newman, *Apologia Pro Vita Sua*, reprint in Fontana Books, London, 1959, p.122.
[2] The standard history is R.W. Church, *The Oxford Movement*, reprinted Chicago, 1970, with introduction by G.F.A. Best. See also S.L. Ollard, *A Short History of the Oxford Movement*, reprinted London, 1963, with introduction by A.M. Allchin. For a more critical approach see W.O. Chadwick, *The Victorian Church*, 2 vols., London, 1966–70, especially vol. I, pp.64–79, 167–221, 250–71, 491–511; vol. II, pp.308–27, 347–58. The most recent short survey is W.N. Yates, *The Oxford Movement and Anglican Ritualism*, Historical Association, London, 1983.

and had allowed the church to become no more than the guardian of the government's corporate religious conscience.[3] The Oxford Movement, in responding to these developments, real or imagined, was thus an inconsistent mixture of the radical and the reactionary, and this fact alone has created difficulties of historical interpretation.

Because the leaders of the Oxford Movement and their disciples sought to change the condition of the Church of England as they found it, they were extremely critical of their predecessors, and this view of the eighteenth and early nineteenth century church is one which has been only too readily accepted by subsequent commentators. Recent research[4] has, however, suggested that the Church of England before the Oxford Movement was not quite the lethargic institution that it has been painted as. It was certainly very different from the church of the late nineteenth and twentieth centuries, but that was largely because the pastoral expectations of its members were very different. In the eighteenth century the clergyman had a social rather than a religious status; the devotional life of the Anglican community was sincere but restrained, doubtful of anything that looked like enthusiasm or exaggerated piety; diocesan administration was efficient and the ill-effects of pluralism and non-residence far less noticeable than the later critics alleged.

The records of Anglican administration, both diocesan and parochial, in Kent as elsewhere, testify to the reasonable state of the church in the eighteenth and early nineteenth centuries. Bishops and archdeacons, at their regular visitations, were extremely diligent in enquiring into the condition of church fabrics, the establishment of parochial charities and libraries, the frequency of church services and numbers of communicants. There survive for the dioceses of both Canterbury and Rochester a large number of inventories of church goods, which show that most churches were properly fitted out with a carpet for the communion table, cushions and hangings for pulpit and reading desk, and all the necessary plate and linen for the proper celebration of Holy Communion. At Rochester cathedral these arrangements are described in considerable detail in an inventory of 1732 (Doc. 1). In most

---

[3] Some of these themes are explored by W.R. Ward, *Religion and Society in England 1790–1850*, London, 1972, and A.D. Gilbert, *Religion and Society in Industrial England*, London, 1976.

[4] Led by N. Sykes, *Church and State in England in the Eighteenth Century*, Cambridge, 1934; useful recent studies are D. McClatchey, *Oxfordshire Clergy 1777–1869*, Oxford, 1960, and J. Obelkevich, *Religion and Rural Society: South Lindsey 1825–1875*, Oxford, 1976.

churches in the larger towns Holy Communion was celebrated monthly, but in the smaller rural parishes quarterly was the norm; celebrations more frequently than once a month and daily services in church were exceptional, though many churches had occasional weekday services in Advent or Lent or on the major fasts and festivals. Confirmations were held at infrequent intervals and vast numbers confirmed (Doc. 2), but this was largely the result of travelling difficulties for bishops, and it is worth noticing that the greater frequency of confirmations after 1830 coincided exactly with the extension of the railways. The fact that most church services were non-sacramental led to a substantial re-arrangement of churches in the eighteenth century. The morning service consisted of Morning Prayer, Litany and Ante-Communion, with a long sermon; though the afternoon service was a little shorter it usually lasted for the best part of two hours. The re-arrangement usually involved the construction of a three-decker pulpit, consisting of pulpit, reading desk and clerk's seat, surrounded by box pews, ranging from ones of considerable comfort for the wealthier families down to much simpler ones, and sometimes even crude benches, for the poorer inhabitants. The pews were usually numbered and assigned to a particular property in the parish, the occupants of which could use the pew for themselves, their guests and their servants. The communion table was effectively closed off from the rest of the church and surrounded by an empty space in which the communicants could gather on sacrament days. These arrangements are clearly shown in a surviving plan of Chiddingstone church in 1724 (Illus. 1). When additional accommodation was required for seating purposes the normal practice was to build one or more galleries into the church to provide this. These galleries were often reached by outside staircases. Normally pews were appropriated to particular properties but in many town churches, where this was obviously inconvenient, it was customary to rent out the seats for fixed annual payments. Seats in churches were therefore considered to be as much a person's private property, either freehold or leasehold, as his house, a practice much condemned by ecclesiastical reformers in the early nineteenth century (Doc. 3). Although the indications are that the liturgy was celebrated with considerable dignity in most eighteenth century churches, there is no doubt that the services were long and uneventful. The range of church music was limited. Only a few churches had organs, and most had to rely on small amateur orchestras whose repertoire consisted of little more than metrical psalms, some settings of other scriptural passages and a few simple hymns. Music books for a small number of parishes, including, in Kent, Kemsing and Trottiscliffe,[5] still survive.

In terms of churchmanship, the Church of England in the first quarter of the nineteenth century consisted largely of three groupings of very unequal size. By far the dominant group, at least in numerical terms, were the conservative 'high churchmen', the so-called 'high and dry' school. They were the successors of the 'high churchmen' who had dominated the Church of England after the restoration of the monarchy in 1660 and who had survived the non-juring schism of the 1690's. In doctrine they supported the apostolic succession, the Prayer Book Liturgy and the connection between church and state. They were sacramentalists though they did not emphasise this much. They regarded political reform and religious enthusiasm with almost equal distaste. They had many friends among the bishops, their champion on the eve of the Oxford Movement being Henry Phillpotts, bishop of Exeter 1830–69. The two smaller groups of churchmen were the erastians and the evangelicals. The erastians were those whose theological opinions, if they had any, tended towards the fashionable rationalism of the eighteenth century, but who were primarily concerned to maintain the union between church and state even if this meant the former operating in effect as a department of the latter. Later on many men of this outlook were attracted by German biblical criticism and theological liberalism. The evangelicals were a rising party in the church in the early nineteenth century. The evangelical movement within eighteenth century Anglicanism had its counterpart in Northern Europe in Lutheran pietism; in England, and even more in Wales, it became fragmented as a result of opposition from the other parties in the church. Part gradually withdrew from the Church of England to form the nucleus of the various Methodist sects. In Kent, where Evangelicalism was generally weak, Vincent Perronet, vicar of Shoreham 1728–85, was a strong supporter of Methodism. Those evangelicals who remained in the Church of England exercised a strong influence on the Anglican revival of the nineteenth century; they were strong in their support of Sunday schools, popular religious literature, parochial charities, more frequent communion services and various

[5] KAO, P205/1/8 and P373/28/1–3.

programmes of political and social reform, a position not unlike that later adopted by the Tractarians. But they also believed in the fundamental importance of the personal conversion experience and the primacy of Scripture, with the result that they were the champions of neither episcopacy nor the Book of Common Prayer. Before 1830 only three Evangelicals had become bishops, though one of these was to be translated to Canterbury in 1848.

The event that really launched the Oxford Movement was the publication of the *Tracts for the Times*, ninety of which appeared between 1833 and 1841. The first paper was a rousing defence of the doctrine of the apostolic succession (Doc. 4). The Oxford Movement attracted its early leaders from both the old-fashioned 'high churchmen' and former Evangelicals in the church, Froude and Keble being among the former, Newman and the Wilberforces among the latter. Only Pusey among the early leaders had had any contact with the liberals and his was only a brief sojourn among the German biblical critics. In its early stages the Oxford Movement was generally viewed with sympathy by most 'high churchmen' for its re-statement of traditional 'high church' values and its defence of the clergy against the encroachments of a secularised and Whig government. The erastians and liberals, led by Thomas Arnold and Sidney Smith, were initially and consistently hostile. The Evangelicals began by sitting on the fence but soon came down against the movement when its romanising tendencies became apparent. Indeed it was this that was the movement's undoing, for the one thing that had brought together Anglican churchmen of all different shades of opinion in the 1820's had been their underlying fear and hatred of Rome. 'The Church of England was emphatically a Protestant church. . . . . Everyone wanted the Church to be Protestant, and everyone was certain that it was Protestant. . . . . When it is to everyone's interest to ignore an obvious fact, it can remain in obscurity for a long time'. It was after 1830 'before anyone pointed out that the formularies of the Church of England are not Protestant at all; that its creeds are identical with those of the Roman church; that bishops were supposed to have a religious function, and not just to sit in the House of Lords and bow down to the Royal Family; and that practices, which Protestants held in horror, such as auricular confession, are advised by the Prayer Book. When the Tractarians drew attention to these and other facts, which were quite undeniable, a large part of the public was outraged. And this is what we should expect; for people do not mind being told what they do not know. They mind being told what they know and will not admit. They minded, for instance, being told by Ibsen, in *Ghosts*, that venereal disease may be hereditary'.[6]

Although the Oxford Movement had begun in the common rooms of the university, and had been pre-eminently theological in its outlook, it did not remain either for long. It had begun by the late 1830's to have an impact in the parishes, and to develop from pure theology to embrace the liturgical and pastoral consequences of that theology. And indeed that is what we should have expected, for Oxford and Cambridge were the training grounds for most of the clergy and the sons of those laymen who were the patrons of ecclesiastical benefices. It was not long before sympathetic 'high churchmen' began to acquire Tractarian curates, and the patrons of livings to offer preferment to their, or their sons', contemporaries at the university. The three phases that marked the progression of the Oxford Movement from the university to the world outside can be conveniently labelled ecclesiology, tractarianism and ritualism. The first two went hand in hand; the last was a later but logical development from the first two. 'Historians have often alleged that there was no continuity between Tractarianism and so-called Ritualism, but Ritualism was an inevitable development of Tractarian piety. The original university Tractarians had stressed the doctrine of the real presence of Christ in the eucharistic elements; in the second generation, men like Arthur Stanton carried this dogmatic truth into the worship of the local parish church. . . . . The claim of the old generation that they had the authority to halt the development of Tractarianism was a political one; it depended on Pusey's judgement of what was negotiable. One ought not to chop off the history of Anglo-Catholicism at the point at which Ritualism appears; the deep disagreement between Evangelical and Ritualist, which cannot simply be reduced to questions of ceremonial, may be inconvenient to a late twentieth century ecumenical interpretation of nineteenth century British church history, but this is not sufficient reason for smothering it'.[7]

Ecclesiology

The earliest parochial manifestation of the Oxford Movement was the campaign for the restoration of old churches and the building of new ones along medievalist lines. The eighteenth century fittings were to be

[6] *Religious Controversies of the Nineteenth Century*, ed. A.O.J. Cockshut, London, 1966, pp.1–2.

[7] J. Kent, *Holding the Fort*, London, 1978, pp.264, 277.

swept away and churches were to be restored to what it was thought they looked like in the thirteenth or fourteenth centuries (Illus. 2). The leading lights in this campaign were the members of the Cambridge Camden Society and the Oxford Society for Promoting the Study of Gothic Architecture, both of which were founded in 1839.[8] One of the earliest textbooks for fellow architects was James Barr's *Anglican Church Architecture*, dedicated to the members of the latter body (Doc. 5). The earliest Kentish exponent of ecclesiology was A.J. Beresford Hope, a member of the Cambridge Camden Society, who had been elected member of Parliament for Maidstone in 1841. His stepfather, Viscount Beresford, had in 1839 commissioned Anthony Salvin to design him a basic chapel of ease on his estate. Christ Church, Kilndown, was a typical, functional, box-shaped, small church of the period until Beresford Hope persuaded his stepfather to allow him to enrich the interior. The results, so graphically described in the Cambridge Camden Society's own journal, *The Ecclesiologist* (Doc. 10), and in a letter from their begetter to Gladstone (Doc. 11), have survived virtually intact (Illus. 3), as have the office books, bound in red morocco with brass mounts, presented by Beresford Hope in 1843. The fittings include a stone altar on three steps, designed by Salvin, rood screen and stalls by R.C. Carpenter, lectern and coronas by William Butterfield, and pulpit modelled on the medieval one in the monastic refectory at Beaulieu. Both Carpenter and Butterfield were 'high churchmen', much approved of by the Camdenians. Butterfield was employed again by Beresford Hope on his second Kentish project, St. Augustine's College at Canterbury, and later on as the architect of All Saints, Margaret Street, in St. Marylebone. Beresford Hope bought the site of the medieval St. Augustine's Abbey at Canterbury in 1844, and reconstructed parts of the monastic buildings to serve as a college for training Anglican missionaries for work overseas. The college was opened in 1848 and was from the start run according to Tractarian principles. An almost contemporary and comparable reconstruction of a monastic building was achieved by Thomas Willement, the student of heraldry and painter of stained glass, in 1845–9, at Davington Priory, Faversham. Another interesting early ecclesiological ensemble of 1848–50 survives in the chancel fittings at Boughton Malherbe.

[8] See J.F. White, *The Cambridge Movement*, Cambridge, 1962; P.F. Anson, *Fashions in Church Furnishings*, rev. ed. London, 1965; B.F.L. Clarke, *Church Builders of the Nineteenth Century*, rev. ed. Newton Abbot, 1969; G.W.O. Addleshaw and F. Etchells, *The Architectural Setting of Anglican Worship*, London, 1950.

Thereafter, the pace of church restoration quickened. That inde-
fatigable visitor of churches, and personal friend of Beresford Hope, Sir
Stephen Glynne, noted with approval early restorations at Westerham
(1850), Thanington (1851), Upchurch (1852), Egerton and Sundridge
(1854), Chevening and Woodchurch (1859).[9] By the end of the century
all but a handful of Kentish churches had been restored, some much
more successfully than others. The restorations were usually, as at
Chislehurst (Docs. 12–14), the work of a special committee set up for
that purpose. Sometimes, as at Shorne,[10] very substantial records of
these proceedings survive, not only the minutes of the restoration
committee, but the correspondence between the committee and the
architect, receipted bills, lists of subscribers to the restoration appeal,
posters for the re-opening of the restored building, orders of service,
menus and tickets for the luncheon held afterwards, and press cuttings
of the whole proceedings.

Despite its proximity to London, relatively few church restorations
or new church buildings in Kent were the work of the major church
architects of the period, many of whom, such as Butterfield and Street,
Bodley and Pearson, were also committed 'high churchmen'. In
addition to his work at Canterbury and Kilndown, Butterfield restored
the churches at Thanington (1846), Great Mongeham (1851),
Godmersham (1865–6) and Milstead (1872), and he completely rebuilt
the church at Langley in 1853–5 for W.B. Pusey, younger brother of the
Tractarian leader, who was rector of this small country parish from
1843 until 1886. Street was responsible for the major restoration at
Stone-next-Dartford, another Tractarian parish, in 1859–60 (Doc. 21),
and for smaller scale restorations at Otford (1863) and High Halden
(1868). Bodley's only major work in Kent was his virtual rebuilding of
Bicknor in 1859–61, his drawings of which include important illustrations of the previous building (Illus. 6–7). Pearson restored All
Saints, Maidstone, in 1886–96, East Farleigh in 1891 (Illus. 4) and the
west front of Rochester Cathedral in 1888–9. However, the major
restoration work done at Rochester, including the new organ case
(Illus. 10), was the responsibility of Sir George Gilbert Scott. Scott,
though converted to ecclesiology, remained an Evangelical but still
received many commissions from 'high churchmen'. He, or perhaps
one should say his office, received more ecclesiastical commissions than

[9] *Notes on the Churches of Kent*, London, 1877, pp.155–6, 169, 176–7, 212–3, 281, 303,
346.
[10] KAO, P336/8/3–6.

any other Victorian architect, including several in Kent. His restorations include Frinsted (1870), where the chancel and north chapel were given elaborate wall decorations which still survive, and the virtual rebuilding of St. Mary de Castro at Dover in 1860–2; his new churches include those of Christ Church, Ramsgate (1846–7); St. Gregory, Canterbury (1848), a memorial to Archbishop Howley; Langton Green (1862–4) and Underriver (1870–5). There is, however, no getting away from the fact that by far the best 'ecclesiological' church in Kent was not an Anglican one at all, but the one built by A.W.N. Pugin, an early convert to Roman Catholicism, next door to his house in Ramsgate. Pugin was the most influential of all the ecclesiologists, and though he had left the Church of England before the formation of the Cambridge Camden society, he strongly supported the ideas of the Camdenians in his writings. St. Augustine's, Ramsgate, with its surviving contemporary plate and vestments, is a church which actually achieved the sort of ideal that Beresford Hope and his colleagues were aiming at.

It has to be admitted that a substantial number of 'ecclesiological' restorations, particularly those by lesser architects, were very heavy-handed. By the end of the nineteenth century a more sensitive approach to church restoration had evolved, particularly among the 'high church' architects and their clerical clients. Two good Anglo-Catholic restorations of this type were those at Elham (1907–11) by F.C. Eden and Kemsing (1900–2) by Sir Ninian Comper. Comper's restoration at Kemsing was the end of a thirty year programme of rebuilding and refurbishing. Prior to 1870 the church had the sort of 'unrestored' interior that now only survives in a handful of Kent churches (Badles—mere, Brookland, Fairfield, Fordwich, Old Romney, Stelling). Then a fairly uninspired restoration took place, followed by the addition of a north aisle in 1890–1, and completed by Comper's extremely tasteful fittings. It is interesting to compare the photographs of the interior in 1870 with those taken from an almost identical position forty years later (Illus. 8–9).

Tractarianism

It would be a mistake to assume that the ecclesiologists were solely, or even primarily, concerned with matters of church architecture. Churches were designed in a particular style because they were intended to serve a particular function. The churches designed by or for the ecclesiologists were designed to permit the liturgical expression of those traditional Catholic doctrines that had been so clearly defended in the

Tracts for the Times. Liturgical innovation, however, was a more complex issue, and contributed to very much greater hostility on the part of the laity, than the restoration of churches, which could be seen as simply a question of decency and good taste. The early Tractarians therefore moved very slowly and cautiously in these areas, a fact which has frequently misled historians into believing that they had little interest in liturgical matters.

Two Kentish parishes in which Tractarian ideals were upheld at an early date were Chislehurst and East Farleigh, and they are good examples of the contrasts that existed between such experiments. Francis Murray (1820–1902),[11] rector of Chislehurst from 1846 until his death, belonged to an aristocratic, traditional 'high church' family, his father, George Murray, being bishop of Rochester 1827–60. Robert and Henry Wilberforce, both of whom held the living of East Farleigh for short periods, were the sons of William Wilberforce, the Evangelical politician and social reformer, and both eventually became Roman Catholics. Another brother, Samuel, also in holy orders and a 'high churchman', remained an Anglican, becoming bishop of Oxford and, later, Winchester. Murray and the Wilberforces were representative of the appeal that the Oxford Movement made to people brought up in very different theological traditions.

Francis Murray has left an interesting memoir of the way in which he cautiously attempted to implement the liturgical expression of Tractarian theology in his parish (Doc. 28). Murray followed in his own career the theological development of the Oxford Movement and Chislehurst became eventually one of the leading centres of ritualist activity in the diocese of Canterbury. Yet, despite his caution, Murray's doctrinal teaching, especially on the Eucharist and confession (Doc. 20), led to petitions against him to Archbishops Longley and Tait. Murray, however, was popular with his parishioners (Doc. 23), and his deliberate policy of moderation, even in matters on which he took a very definite theological standpoint, ensured that he was never in serious trouble with the ecclesiastical authorities.

Very much more serious divisions took place at East Farleigh. Robert Wilberforce (1802–57) became vicar of East Farleigh in 1832, exchanging the living for that of Burton Agnes in Yorkshire in 1840; he became archdeacon of the East Riding in 1841, but resigned all his

---

[11] For a detailed study of Francis Murray see the present writer's forthcoming article in *Archaeologia Cantiana*, xcviii (1982).

preferment in 1854 to become a Roman Catholic. At East Farleigh he seems to have made a few liturgical changes which were abolished by his successor C.H. Lutwidge (1840–3). Henry Wilberforce (1807–73) succeeded to East Farleigh in 1843 and resigned the living shortly before he also became a Roman Catholic in 1850. Henry Wilberforce had been a pupil of Newman, who had encouraged him to take holy orders. He became perpetual curate of Bransgore in Hampshire in 1834, and moved to Kent to become vicar of Walmer in 1841. The opposition to him began immediately after the announcement of his preferment to East Farleigh, much of it organised by Stephen Jenner, who had been Lutwidge's curate. Apparently, Lutwidge had shortly before his death given Jenner notice to find another curacy, but Jenner had hoped that after Lutwidge's death he might instead be offered the living, one of the richest in the county. When Wilberforce was appointed, Jenner offered to continue as his curate, but Wilberforce told him that he preferred to abide by Lutwidge's previous arrangements. There is no evidence to suggest that Jenner was an Evangelical or particularly anti-Tractarian in his views. His opposition to Wilberforce seems to have been based entirely on personal disappointment, but he very carefully used the evidence of Wilberforce's known 'high church' connections and suspected 'high church' opinions to stir up public opinion against him. It was alleged that Wilberforce had made liturgical innovations in his previous parishes, but Wilberforce claimed that, on the contrary, he had left the services 'as I found them, although in each case much more frequently performed than before'.[12] Consequently when Wilberforce arrived at East Farleigh he found that he had a ready-made opposition party to contend with, so that when he rather unwisely attempted to restore some of the liturgical practices introduced by his brother, there was a public outcry. Allegations in the newspapers and a petition to Archbishop Howley (Doc. 7), resulted in an enquiry conducted initially by John Griffith, vicar of Boxley and canon of Rochester, and a formal judgement on the conflict by the then archdeacon of Maidstone, and future dean of Canterbury, William Lyall (Doc. 8). Although both Lyall and Howley sided very clearly with Wilberforce, this did not put an end to the acrimonious divisions

---

[12] H. Wilberforce, *Facts and Documents Relating to East Farleigh*, London, 1845, p.11.

in the parish, and there was a lengthy correspondence between the archbishop, the vicar and his former churchwarden, Gabriel Kennard (Doc. 9).

In the end, however, it was national rather than local circumstances which brought about Henry Wilberforce's departure from East Farleigh. The short period within which the Tractarians had been upheld as the defenders of the liberties of the Church of England passed quickly. The publication of Froude's *Remains*, with its vehement denunciations of the English Reformation and its indiscreet revelations of the author's personal doubts and mortifications, and, even more, the publication of Newman's *Tract XC*, which argued that there was nothing in the official formularies of the Church of England inconsistent with the decrees of the Council of Trent, offended the deep Protestantism of most English churchmen, 'high', 'low' or 'broad'. By the early 1840's there were vigorous conflicts between the Evangelicals and the Tractarians over the doctrine of baptismal regeneration (Doc. 6), which eventually resulted in a Privy Council judgement appearing to favour the former. The increasing isolation of the more committed Tractarians began to make many of them, especially those who had not come from traditional 'high church' backgrounds, question the theological basis of their position within the Church of England and to conclude that they ought to become Roman Catholics. Protestant churchmen, though publicly horrified, were privately delighted; the Tractarians could with impunity be denounced as 'Romanisers'. Those Tractarians who regarded themselves as restoring the Church of England to the liturgical and theological standards of the seventeenth century were dejected. More moderate 'high churchmen', who had enthusiastically supported the Tractarians in the 1830's, began to distance themselves from the leaders of that party in the 1840's. A good Kentish example is Benjamin Harrison, Archdeacon of Maidstone 1845–87, who had written four of the early tracts, but who took little or no part in the later phases of the Oxford Movement. A slow trickle of secessions to Rome had begun by 1840, but it became rather more like a flood after Newman and several of his closest associates became Roman Catholics in 1845. Thereafter every new religious crisis, in which the Catholic position within the Church of England seemed to be weakened by adverse legal judgements, political legislation or episcopal persecution, resulted in another batch of secessions. These secessions, and public hostility towards the restoration of the Roman Catholic hierarchy in 1850, led to a wave of hysterical anti-Roman Catholic and anti-Tractarian propaganda, in the decade that followed (Docs. 16, 18 and 19).[13]

Henry Wilberforce, as a former pupil and a continuing close friend of Newman, found himself under intense pressure to follow his example. As early as 1846 Newman hoped that Wilberforce might secede, but he was persuaded against it by the fact that Keble, Manning and Pusey were prepared to remain in the Church of England.[14] On 1 October 1849 Newman wrote to Wilberforce: 'I think I quite understand your state of mind, and earnestly trust and believe that God is leading you forward to the sure rest of His True Fold. . . . Keep before your mind that, when you are convinced, you must act . . . . . you will have a great deal to go through. I do not undervalue it — but in proportion to your suffering, will be your reward. . . . O the joy it will be to me to see you and embrace you as the Patriarch turned himself with yearning heart to his lost son. . . . . I shall say Mass for you three days'.[15] Newman did not have long to wait. The cholera epidemic of 1849 and the Gorham Judgement on baptismal regeneration eventually persuaded Wilberforce's wife to secede in June 1850. A month later Wilberforce announced that he would resign his living, and he was received into the Roman Catholic church in November 1850.[16] A few months later he wrote a deeply moving letter to his former parishioners, explaining why he had taken the decision he had and recommending that those who could in conscience do so should follow him (Doc. 17).

The effect on the parish was clearly considerable. One of Wilberforce's last acts at East Farleigh had been to establish one of the hallmarks of parochial Tractarianism, a surpliced choir, and this provoked considerable conflict after his secession (Doc. 15), between those who had been his supporters and those who had led the opposition to him in 1843–4. Clearly his supporters had to admit eventual defeat but not without a considerable struggle to maintain Tractarian traditions in the celebration of divine service. It is an interesting illustration of the fact that, though Tractarian clergy were certainly unpopular with many sections of the laity, there was a vigorous pro-Tractarian lobby which was not just confined to the ranks of the clergy.

Another interesting early example of the parochial impact of the Oxford Movement can be seen at Gravesend where the proprietory

[13] See also E.R. Norman, *Anti-Catholicism in Victorian England*, London, 1968.
[14] *Letters and Diaries of John Henry Newman*, xi, pp.210, 215.
[15] *Ibid.*, xiii, pp.266–7.
[16] *Ibid.*, xiii, pp.260, 287, 477: xiv, pp.3, 71.

chapel of St. John was purchased by a Tractarian clergyman, William John Blew (1808–94), in 1842. Blew introduced daily choral services and built up a strong local following. In April 1851, in the aftermath of the 'Papal Aggression' crisis, Blew was inhibited by Bishop Murray of Rochester from preaching for six months, because of his declared support for the restoration of the Roman Catholic hierarchy. He reacted by selling the church, which was his private property, to the then newly established Roman Catholic diocese of Southwark and it was re-opened in October 1851 as a Roman Catholic chapel. Blew himself, though he attended this ceremony, remained an Anglican. Some of his former congregation became Roman Catholics, and the remainder formed the nucleus of the congregation of Christ Church, Gravesend, consecrated in 1856, which maintained the liturgical tradition begun at St. John's.[17]

After 1850 a number of other Kentish parishes began to adopt a Tractarian outlook. One such was Rolvenden during the incumbency of John William Rumsey (1855–84), for which the surviving service registers provide a detailed account of what was both attempted and achieved (Doc. 22). What is interesting is the way in which Rumsey managed to achieve very respectable congregations for both his daily and his Sunday services, in a rural parish and at a time when such innovations were the exception rather than the rule. Another rural parish with a strong Tractarian tradition was Christ Church, Kilndown, where services had been developed to complement Beresford Hope's ecclesiological fittings. By 1874 there was a celebration of Holy Communion every Sunday and Holy Day, the eastward position was taken by the celebrant who wore linen vestments, and the altar candles were lighted.[18] By the end of the century a number of other rural parishes had also become centres of Tractarian activity, though even fairly moderate innovations, such as those at Aylesford (Doc. 29), could cause a certain amount of parochial tension. Even if incumbents were unwilling to risk the conflicts produced by liturgical innovation, they could, as at East Malling (Illus. 14), decorate the interiors of their churches in such a way as to make their Tractarian outlook abundantly clear to the initiated.

---

[17] R.H. Hiscock, 'The Proprietory Chapel of St. John, Gravesend', *Archaeologia Cantiana* xciii (1977), pp.1–24.
[18] *Tourists' Church Guide*, London, 1874.

Ritualism

After the various crises of the 1840's and 1850's 'high churchmen' began to regain their confidence and to experiment further. It is to some extent a matter of opinion as to whether the early Tractarians realised the full import of the direction in which their teachings would lead. Certainly by the time the Oxford Movement had reached what might be termed its second generation, the implications could no longer be ignored. The decision that had to be taken was in effect where to apply the brake. The early Tractarians had endeavoured to assert that just because the Church of England had ceased to be in communion with the bishop of Rome, this did not mean that she had ceased to be part of the Catholic church, and that the present need was to re-emphasise that Catholicity and to modify the view of the church as a Protestant one. But what in reality did this mean? Here the Tractarians were divided and it was when they attempted to answer the question that the divisions became apparent and sometimes acrimonious. Some felt that the ideal was to re-establish the Church of England as it had been in the seventeenth century. Others preferred to return to an earlier, medieval, model, before the breach with Rome, but removing the various corrupt practices that had caused the breach. A minority believed that simply trying to return to some kind of ecclesiastical golden age was a nonsense, and that what was needed was to take into Anglicanism all that was acceptable within modern Roman Catholicism in the hope that eventually the two churches would be re-united.

The first signs of growing Tractarian confidence were the establishment of religious orders for men and women, the founding of various societies to promote 'high church' causes and the development of parochial ritualism.[19] Kent was not a major centre of monastic activity, though the Clewer sisters ran a convalescent home and mission to the poor in Folkestone, and a community of Benedictine nuns moved to West Malling in 1893 (Doc. 30). All the major 'high church' societies had members or local branches in Kentish parishes: the English Church Union, which acted as the principal defender of clergy under Protestant attack; the Society of the Holy Cross, which was the principal promoter of retreats and auricular confession; the Confraternity of the Blessed Sacrament, which encouraged the exaltation of

[19] On Anglican Monasticism see P.F. Anson, *The Call of the Cloister*, rev. ed. London, 1964: there is no good modern study of either the 'high church' societies or parochial ritualism, but much of the evidence is presented for condemnation in W. Walsh, *Secret History of the Oxford Movement*, London, 1897.

the Eucharist; and the Guild of All Souls, which organised prayers for the faithful departed. A number of other wider church organisations, such as the Additional Curates Society, the Universities' Mission to Central Africa and the Church of England Working Men's Society, were either founded by 'high churchmen' or largely dominated by them. Parochial ritualism had begun to emerge in Kent after 1860, its major early centre being the seaside resort of Folkestone. Seaside resorts have a somewhat undeserved reputation, or notoriety, in this context. Other seaside centres of ritualist activity included Brighton, Scarborough and Torquay.[20] But there were seaside resorts that were not so affected, and in Kent this was certainly the case at Margate, though it might have been different if J.L. Lyne's (*alias* Father Ignatius') negotiations towards securing a curacy there had not proved abortive.[21]

The development of Folkestone as the early centre of Kentish ritualism was the result of the appointment of Matthew Woodward (Illus. 11) to the vicarage of the parish church in 1851. When he was appointed he had the reputation of being an Evangelical,[22] and his adoption of a fairly elaborate ritual at the parish church, and his promotion of a very much more extravagant ritual at some of its daughter churches, were regarded as a betrayal by a fair number of his parishioners. The development of parochial ritualism had been given considerable encouragement by the publication of John Purchas' *Directorium Anglicanum* in 1858 (Illus. 5). This showed Anglican clergy how they could manage to integrate traditional Catholic ceremonial into the services of the Book of Common Prayer. When such practices began to be condemned by both the bishops and the courts, ritualists were encouraged by bodies such as the English Church Union to insist on the minimum of what were termed the six points: eastward position, mixed chalice, wafer bread, lighted candles, vestments and incense. It was felt that these and other practices were legitimised by a literal interpretation of the ornaments rubric, which ordered that in liturgical matters the Church of England should abide by what was the practice in the second year of the reign of Edward VI (1548–9), even though the rubric had not been so interpreted over the previous three centuries.

[20] See the present writer's forthcoming article, 'Bells and Smells: London, Brighton and South Coast Religion Reconsidered', in *Southern History* V (1983).

[21] Lambeth Palace Library, Longley Papers, vol. 4, ff.146–54, 213–18.

[22] Editorial in *Folkestone Chronicle*, 3 October 1863: 'The Parishioners know only too well how that when he came among them twelve years ago, his professions were of an Evangelical tendency, at which time he strongly objected to any of those peculiar views he is now seeking to introduce'.

Central to Woodward's liturgical innovations and pastoral activity was the complete refurbishing of the parish church, and the building of new churches in a rapidly developing town. The nave and north aisle of the parish church were rebuilt and the north transept extended in 1856–9. The south chancel aisle and south transept were rebuilt in 1869, and the south aisle in 1874. The sanctuary was completely remodelled with arcading and reredos in alabaster and Devon marble in 1885 (Illus. 13), and between 1889 and 1901 the nave and aisles were painted with various narrative scenes, including the Stations of the Cross (Illus. 12). Four daughter churches were built of which three survive: St. Peter (1862–4), Holy Trinity (1868–9) and St. Saviour (1891–2). The conflict over the ritual in Woodward's churches began in earnest in 1862 after he had introduced the Tractarian *Hymns Ancient and Modern* at the parish church. Thereafter the local newspapers are full of correspondence, editorials and reports on the latest ecclesiastical intelligence. The attacks are on Woodward himself and his principal protegés, C.J. Ridsdale, vicar of St. Peter's 1868–1923, and E. Husband, curate-in-charge and vicar of St. Michael's 1872–1908. Leading the attack was the ultra-Protestant *Folkestone Observer*. The editors of the *Folkestone Chronicle* and *Folkestone Express*, though opposed to ritualism, at least recognised that Woodward, Ridsdale and Husband were dedicated and effective parish priests. The Church Association, a national body founded in 1865 to promote the suppression of ritualism, decided that its principal target in Folkestone would be Ridsdale, even though both Husband and Woodward had clearly indulged in practices that the courts were likely to declare illegal. Accordingly the Association arranged for local inhabitants to promote a suit against Ridsdale. An attempt made in 1873 to force Ridsdale to remove the Stations of the Cross in St. Peter's failed. Two years later, however, a new suit against Ridsdale was initiated under the provisions of the new Public Worship Regulation Act. This act had been the brainchild of Archbishop Tait and represented a compromise between the bishops and the strongly anti-ritualist politicians, such as Cairns and Shaftesbury. The act provided that any three 'aggrieved parishioners' could initiate a suit against an incumbent who was thought to be in breach of the law in his liturgical practices. Whilst Ridsdale was on his honeymoon, after his marriage to Matthew Woodward's eldest daughter, the Church Association organised the necessary complaints. Ridsdale's supporters claimed that the complainants, though resident in St. Peter's parish, were not regular worshippers at their parish church, the congregation of which was solidly behind Ridsdale, and that one of them had offered to withdraw his evidence for the sum of £200. The allegations made against Ridsdale included his use of the eastward position, eucharistic vestments and wafer bread. Ritualists were divided as to what action to take in response to the new legislation. Some simply refused to acknowledge the jurisdiction of a secular court. Ridsdale, however, decided to defend the action and his expenses were defrayed by the English Church Union, both sides employing eminent lawyers. Not surprisingly the judgement went against Ridsdale and he decided to appeal to the Judicial Committee of the Privy Council. In the meantime he announced that he would discontinue all celebrations of Holy Communion at St. Peter's while the judgement of the lower court stood. In May 1877 Ridsdale learned that he had effectively lost his appeal. Vestments were declared illegal. So was wafer bread, though the court ruled that the complainants had not proved conclusively that Ridsdale had used it. The eastward position was only permitted provided that the manual acts of breaking the bread and taking the cup could be clearly seen by the congregation. In the aftermath of the judgement, and bombarded by conflicting advice (Doc. 24), Ridsdale dithered. He eventually reached a compromise with Tait, whereby the archbishop in effect granted him a dispensation from the ornaments rubric which Ridsdale believed to order the use of vestments.[23]

Although Ridsdale was unpopular with many of his fellow ritualists, who felt he had betrayed them at a time when others, such as S.F. Green, who later became vicar of Charlton-in-Dover, and a former Folkestone curate, Arthur Tooth, were prepared to go to prison rather than obey the courts, his actions had the effect of taking much of the steam out of the ritualist controversies in Folkestone. The town remained a centre of ritualist activity; indeed the number of ritualist churches had increased from three to five by the mid-1880's. Some Evangelicals felt so disheartened that they seceded from the Church of England to form their own independent congregation with a liturgy totally purged of popish error (Doc. 27). But there had been some further secessions to Rome as well, including that of Matthew Woodward's own wife.

The attacks on the ritualists, however, left their mark. They produced very much a ghetto mentality among Anglo-Catholics which

[23] Full summary of the judgement and its implications in P.T. Marsh, *The Victorian Church in Decline*, London, 1969, pp.220–5, and J. Bentley, *Ritualism and Politics in Victorian Britain*, Oxford, 1978, pp.97–100.

lasted for many years, and indeed to some extent still exists. They went to endless lengths to ensure that the liturgical innovations they had fought for would be safe-guarded. At Folkestone a trust deed was drawn up to protect the eucharistic vestments (Doc. 31). At Tunbridge Wells, despite Evangelical protestations (Doc. 25), the patronage of the new ritualist church of St. Barnabas (Illus. 15) was vested in trustees who could be relied upon to present Anglo-Catholic incumbents. Such incumbents went out of their way to fill their churches with ornaments which would both demonstrate to the world their vigorous Catholicity, whilst at the same time embarrassing any future incumbent who might be tempted to be 'Church of England', to Anglo-Catholics of that generation a phrase of the utmost contempt. Those who fitted out St. Nicholas, Chislehurst (Doc. 26), or Holy Trinity, Broadstairs (Illus. 16), had no interest in promoting the Anglican *via media* of the more conservative 'high churchmen'.[24]

The first quarter of the twentieth century was the high water mark of the Catholic Revival in the Church of England. In 1906 the Royal Commission on Ecclesiastical Discipline (Doc. 32) admitted that the attempts to apply a brake to ritualism, either by the bishops or through the courts, had failed. Although Anglo-Catholics had plenty of opponents, they also had powerful friends. Some bishops had always been, even if only secretly, sympathetic; there was a vigorous 'high church' lobby in both Houses of Parliament, and among the ranks of the principal landed families; there was the popular support which individual clergymen were able to count on from loyal congregations. Although even in the 1920's and 1930's there continued to be attempts by the bishops and others to control the more advanced Anglo-Catholic practices, the limits of what was found to be acceptable continued to expand: first vestments, then incense, then reservation of the Blessed Sacrament, ceased to be matters about which it was felt necessary to argue. Many practices which would have been considered dangerously ritualistic even in the 1870's, such as the eastward position or lighted candles or the mixed chalice, had become normal Anglican practice.

The situation in Kent by the beginning of the twentieth century was that a large number of churches had adopted the more moderate liturgical innovations of the ritualists, but that the more extreme ones were limited to about forty churches in the county. In the diocese of Canterbury, which then covered most of Kent, the eastward position

[24] For an anecdotal account of later Anglo-Catholicism see A. Hughes, *Rivers of the Flood*, London, 1961.

was taken in three out of four churches, and in nearly half lighted candles and the mixed chalice were also in use. All the major towns in Kent with the exception of Canterbury, Maidstone and Margate had at least one church in which the eucharistic vestments were worn. They were also used in about twenty rural parishes. The use of incense was, however, restricted to only a handful of urban churches and one rural one, Egerton, which had a ritualist incumbent from 1901 to 1909.[25]

What then had been the contribution of the Oxford Movement to the Church in Kent? Looked at objectively, and despite the frustrations and bitterness that some of the disputes inevitably caused, the established church in Kent was a very different institution in 1900 from what it had been in 1800. Whether this was progress or not is a matter of opinion, though most churchmen thought it was. Services had been increased and were conducted with greater ceremonial; the number of communicants had risen as had the frequency of celebrations; the parishes were better organised pastorally, with many varieties of religious organisations; church fabrics had been repaired and the interiors refitted; the functions and priorities of the clergy had been re-assessed and emphasis placed on the need for vigorous spiritual leadership; in short the church had ceased to be a sort of religious appendage of the state, but had developed a vigorous life and personality of its own, even though it had had to sacrifice much of its former political influence to achieve this. It would be misleading to suggest that the Oxford Movement was solely responsible for all these developments, but it would not be an exaggeration to say that it was the single most important factor in bringing them about.

[25] Statistics from *Ritualistic Clergy List*, London, 1903.

DOCUMENTS

1. *Part of an inventory of goods in Rochester Cathedral taken in 1732* [KAO, DRc/EIf 8]

> This inventory is a particularly detailed account of the furnishings of a church in the mid-eighteenth century, and shows the mixture of decay and decency which typified the Church of England in this period. Lesser churches obviously had much smaller collections of plate and (what were then termed) vestments. Most churches would have had coverings for the altar and hangings for the pulpit, together with a white cloth to cover the altar at celebrations of the Holy Communion and a napkin to cover the elements, and one or more surplices. The survival of candlesticks in parish churches was exceptionally rare.

An Inventory of all ye goods belonging to ye Cathedral Church of Rochester exhibited August ye 9th to ye Rev^d Dr Herring, Dean of ye s^d church by John Robinson preb^y and treas^r of ye s^d church, ano dom. 1732.

In ye Choir
One hanging brass candlestick wth 24 branches and a chain consisting of six iron links painted.
One standing brass eagle desk fashion'd wth basketts, a bible best paper printed anno 1717.
Two large old bibles used at early morning prayers, one of them now at Mr. Gibbon's to be mended.
Twelve Com̄ prayer books for ye dean and preb^s and min^r canons, some of wch are much decay^d.
Six books for ye lay clerks some of them much deccayd.
Seven large Com̄ prayer books bought for ye dean and preb^s anno 1727.
Six Com̄ prayer books for ye min^r canons, bought anno 1730 and six reading desks.
Four quarto prayer books for ye choristers bought anno 1727.
Dr. Crofts' Musica Sacra 2 vol.
Four books, vizt counter tenor, tenor, bass, treble, decay^d, and one large service book for Mr. Dean.
Treble, count^r ten^r, ten^r, bass, Cantoris.
Three books for ye organ.
Six short folios, called Tomkins.

Six cushions wth purple cloth for ye dean and preb^s and 2 purple cloth falls wth silk fringes, and 2 purple velvet valences, over ye stalls of ye dean and vice-dean, and 2 bay curtains, and two iron curtain rodds.
Sixteen cushions for ye seats of ye dean and preb^s.
Fifteen cushions of purple bays in ye mayor, and aldermen and comon council-men's seats, wth 5 falls for ye same wth silk fringe.
Fifteen cushions of purple bays in ye mayor, and aldermen and comon archdeacon's seat.
In ye bishop's seat, one purple velvet cushio wth a velvet fall, and silk fringe, and a sitting cushion of purple bays, and one purple silk curtain wth an iron rodd.
Twenty forms, and a litany desk cover'd wth purple cloth. Eight low forms wth old matts naild on them to kneel on, and one small one at ye litany desk.
Thirty five short brass sockets, and thirty long ones wth broad dishes. A wreath'd candlestick of iron, painted and fixed at ye pulpit, and a blew silk curtain and an iron rodd. Tapistry hangings, form^rly over ye comunion table, and a picture of a Dutch church, ye gift of Dr. Coney. wth in ye altar rails.
Upon ye table one carpet of three breadths, wth crimson velvet, and four of purple silk, brocaded wth gold and silver, two cushions, one side being of the s^d purple silk, lined wth red silk. Two Comon pray^er books, ye gift of Dean Ullock printed anno 1700, and a bible and Comon prayer book, both bound with red velvet.
Two quarto Comon prayer books bound in Morocco leather, gilt, with blue silk strings, fringed wth gold, bought anno dom. 1730.
A sett of black bays covering for ye altar.
An old purple velvet cov'ring for ye Comunion table.
Five hassocks, two new forms Coverd wth red bays.

In ye Treasury.
One great chest, one pair of large gild candlesticks, one large gilt bason, one pair of silver flaggons, one pair of gilt cups, wth gilt covers, one pair of gilt wrought patines, wth one cover to both.
One bason, two flaggons, two large candlesticks, two patines with covers, two chalices with covers, all gilt, with cases for each, being ye gift of Sr Joseph Williamson. A flasket to carry ye plate, one diaper Communion table cloth, and two napkins.

2. *Notes made by the Revd. Thomas Willis, curate of Wateringbury, relating to ecclesiastical events, including a confirmation at Malling on 13 May 1826* [KAO, P385/1/3]

Thomas Willis appears, from the Wateringbury parish registers, to have served as curate to his father, Dr. Thomas Willis, who seems to have been fairly inactive in the parish, between 1825 and 1829. His interest in the detail of liturgical matters is interesting, and he was clearly a moderate reformer, possibly influenced by Evangelicalism. The large and infrequent confirmation services he describes were typical of those held in the pre-railway age when the ability of bishops to travel around their dioceses was severely restricted.

On Saturday the 13th of May 1826, the day before Whitsunday, the Bp. of Rochester himself confirmed at Malling. It was only a confirmation. There was no sermon after but an address before conf[irmation] which the Bp's. Chaplain read out of a pew in which the Bishop was. Prayers were first read by Mr. Bates. The Bp. laid his hands upon four at a time by joining two heads together, and laying one of his hands upon two heads. There were ninety and seven confirmed out of this parish. We were ordered to be at Malling by 10. When the church was filled, the Bp. came in about 11 and service began. The girls filled the Church 1st and were confirmed 1st. The Church was filled twice. The question therefore was put from the Altar twice and 'I do' twice repeated. We had 3 weeks notice of the Confirmation. I distributed, here, the 'order of Confirmation', 'Nelson's Instructions for Confirmation' and Abp. Secker's Sermon on Confirmation, and gave them each a ticket with 'Examined for Confirmation and approved' written on it with my signature. All of which tickets were required in the Church. The Bps. chaplain, viz. one of his sons, officiated within the Altar rails in a surplice and hood.

July 30 1826. The singing in the afternoon service took place today after the second lesson and will continue to do so in future. It was at Colonel Jones's desire that my father altered it to that place instead of after the prayer 'Lighten our darkness'. It is generally approved of there tho' contrary to the rubric.

1826 February 8th. Ash Wednesday. The Sunday School attended at the School previously and went to church. There were Morning Prayers and the Commination.

Christmas Day. Monday. The School attended morning and evening. They did not return after Evening Prayers to School. A Sermon in the morning. I read no Litany it being Monday. Sacrament also. The singers sang one Hymn for the Day, but not the one attached to the New Version of the Psalms. I am determined from this time to refuse their singing any Hymns or Psalms which are not in the authorized versions, the Old and New Versions. I conceive I might as well read a

Psalm not in the Prayer Book, as they sing one not authorized by the Head of our Church.

The 5th of November fell upon a Sunday. I did not read the Gunpowder Treason Service.

The Sittings in the Church.
In the year 1818, 96 Free Sittings were added to the number then existing; and thus the number of Sittings (free and appropriated together) became 340.
In 1824, 270 Sittings more were added by an Enlargement of the Church, of which number, 224 were declared to be *Free for Ever*, in addition to the 96 Free Sittings of the year 1818.
Allowing 18 Inches to a Sitting, The Old Gallery contains 91 Sittings. Underneath it there are 18 Sittings.
The New Gallery contains 40 Sittings.
Under it are 67 Sittings.
The space allotted for the Sunday School in the New Gallery (allowing 15 Inches to a Sitting) contains 104 Sittings.
Total 320. All of which are *Free for Ever*.
Since the Year 1826 the Church has 320 Free Sittings for ever and 290 Appropriated Sittings, 610 in all.
Thos Willis, Feby 7th 1831.

3. *Advertisement to the first volume of the 'Tracts for the Times', published in 1834, and the full text of the first tract, issued in 1833.*

The advertisement is a concise summary of the doctrines for which the early leaders of the Oxford Movement stood, and the first tract in the series is a spirited defence of the most crucial of these doctrines, that of the apostolic succession. Although the leaders of the movement were at this stage largely re-emphasising traditional 'high church' opinions, held throughout the seventeenth and eighteenth centuries, they were doing so in a way calculated to infuriate those who regarded doctrinal matters as being of secondary importance, either to the conversion experience or the corporate solidarity of church and state.

Advertisement to Volume I
The following Tracts were published with the object of contributing something towards the practical revival of doctrines which, although held by the great divines of our Church, at present have become obsolete with the majority of her members, and are withdrawn from

public view even by the more learned and orthodox few who still adhere to them. The Apostolic succession, the Holy Catholic Church, were principles of action in the minds of our predecessors of the seventeenth century; but, in proportion as the maintenance of the Church has been secured by law, her ministers have been under the temptation of leaning on an arm of flesh instead of her own divinely-provided discipline, a temptation increased by political events and arrangements which need not here be more than alluded to. A lamentable increase of sectarianism has followed; being occasioned (in addition to other more obvious causes), first, by the cold aspect which the new Church doctrines have presented to the religious sensibilities of the mind, next to their meagreness in suggesting motives to restrain it from seeking out a more influential discipline. Doubtless obedience to the law of the land, and the careful maintenance of 'decency and order' (the topics in usage among us), are plain duties of the Gospel, and a reasonable ground for keeping in communion with the Established Church; yet, if Providence has graciously provided for our weakness more interesting and constraining motives, it is a sin thanklessly to neglect them; just as it would be a mistake to rest the duties of temperance or justice on the mere law of natural religion, when they are mercifully sanctioned in the Gospel by the more winning authority of our Saviour Christ. Experience has shown the inefficacy of the mere injunctions of Church order, however scripturally enforced, in restraining from schism the awakened and anxious sinner; who goes to a dissenting preacher 'because (as he expresses it) he gets good from him': and though he does not stand excused in God's sight for yielding to the temptation, surely the Ministers of the Church are not blameless if, by keeping back the more gracious and consoling truths provided for the little ones of Christ, they indirectly lead him into it. Had he been taught as a child, that the Sacraments, not preaching, are the sources of Divine Grace; that the Apostolical ministry had a virtue in it which went out over the whole Church, when sought by the prayer of faith; that fellowship with it was a gift and privilege, as well as a duty, we could not have had so many wanderers from our fold, nor so many cold hearts within it.

This instance may suggest many others of the superior *influence* of an apostolical over a mere secular method of teaching. The awakened mind knows its wants, but cannot provide for them; and in its hunger will feed upon ashes, if it cannot obtain the pure milk of the Word. Methodism and Popery are in different ways the refuge of those whom the Church stints of the gift of grace; they are the foster-mothers of abandoned children. The neglect of the daily service, the desecration of festivals, the Eucharist scantily administered, insubordination permitted in all ranks of the Church, orders and offices imperfectly developed, the want of Societies for particular religious objects, and the like deficiencies, lead the feverish mind, desirous of a vent to its feelings, and a stricter rule of life, to the smaller religious Communities, to prayer and bible meetings, and ill-advised institutions and societies, on the one hand, — on the other, to the solemn and captivating services by which Popery gains its proselytes. Moreover, the multitude of men cannot teach or guide themselves; and an injunction given them to depend on their private judgment, cruel in itself, is doubly hurtful, as throwing them on such teachers as speak daringly and promise largely, and not only aid but supersede individual exertion.

These remarks may serve as a clue, for those who care to pursue it, to the views which have led to the publication of the following Tracts. The Church of Christ was intended to cope with human nature in all its forms, and surely the gifts vouchsafed it are adequate for that gracious purpose. There are zealous sons and servants of her English branch, who see with sorrow that she is defrauded of her full usefulness by particular theories and principles of the present age, which interfere with the execution of one portion of her commission; and while they consider that the revival of this portion of truth is especially adapted to break up existing parties in the Church, and to form instead a bond of union among all who love the Lord Jesus Christ in sincerity, they believe that nothing but these neglected doctrines, faithfully preached, will repress that extension of Popery for which the ever-multiplying divisions of the religious world are too clearly preparing the way.

OXFORD, *The Feast of All Saints*, 1834.

TRACT I.   *Thoughts on the Ministerial Commission. Respectfully Addressed to the Clergy*

I am but one of yourselves, — a Presbyter; and therefore I conceal my name, lest I should take too much on myself by speaking in my own person. Yet speak I must; for the times are very evil, yet no one speaks against them.

Is not this so? Do not we 'look one upon another', yet perform nothing? De we not all confess the peril into which the Church is come, yet sit still each in his own retirement, as if mountains and seas cut off brother from brother? Therefore suffer me, while I try to draw you forth from those pleasant retreats which it has been our blessedness hitherto to enjoy, to contemplate the condition and prospects of our Holy Mother in a practical way; so that one and all may unlearn that idle habit, which has grown upon us, of owning the state of things to be bad, yet doing nothing to remedy it.

Consider a moment. Is it fair, is it dutiful, to suffer our Bishops to stand the brunt of the battle without doing our part to support them? Upon them comes 'the care of all the Churches'. This cannot be helped:

indeed it is their glory. Not one of us would wish in the least to deprive them of the duties, the toils, the responsibilities of their high Office. And, black event as it would be for the country, yet (as far as they are concerned) we could not wish them a more blessed termination of their course than the spoiling of their goods, and martyrdom.

To them then we willingly and affectionately relinquish their high privileges and honours; we encroach not upon the rights of the successors of the Apostles; we touch not their sword and crosier. Yet surely we may be their shield-bearers in the battle without offence; and by our voice and deeds be to them what Luke and Timothy were to St. Paul.

Now then let me come at once to the subject which leads me to address you. Should the Government and Country so far forget their God as to cast off the Church, to deprive it of its temporal honours and substance, *on what* will you rest the claim of respect and attention which you make upon your flocks? Hitherto you have been upheld by your birth, your education, your wealth, your connections; should these secular advantages cease, on what must Christ's Ministers depend? Is not this a serious practical question? We know how miserable is the state of religious bodies not supported by the State. Look at the Dissenters on all sides of you, and you will see at once that their Ministers, depending simply upon the people, become the *creatures* of the people. Are you content that this should be your case? Alas! can a greater evil befall Christians than for their teachers to be guided by them, instead of guiding? How can we 'hold fast the form of sound words' and 'keep that which is committed to our trust', if our influence is to depend simply on our popularity? Is it not our very office to *oppose* the world? can we then allow ourselves to *court* it? to preach smooth things and prophesy deceits? to make the way of life easy to the rich and indolent, and to bribe the humbler classes by excitements and strong intoxicating doctrine? Surely it must not be so; — and the question recurs, on *what* are we to rest our authority when the State deserts us?

Christ has not left His Church without claim of its own upon the attention of men. Surely not. Hard Master He cannot be, to bid us oppose the world, yet give us no credentials for so doing. There are some who rest their divine mission on their own unsupported assertion; others, who rest it upon their popularity; others, on their success; and others, who rest it upon their temporal distinctions. This last case has, perhaps, been too much our own; I fear we have neglected the real ground on which our authority is built, — our apostolical descent.

We have been born, not of blood, nor of the will of the flesh, nor of the will of man, but of God. The Lord Jesus Christ gave His Spirit to His Apostles; they in turn laid their hands on those who should succeed them; and these again on others; and so the sacred gift has been handed down to our present Bishops, who have appointed us as their assistants, and in some sense representatives.

Now every one of us believes this. I know that some will at first deny they do; still they do believe it. Only, it is not sufficiently practically impressed on their minds. They *do* believe it; for it is the doctrine of the Ordination Service, which they have recognised as truth in the most solemn season of their lives. In order, then, not to prove, but to remind and impress, I entreat your attention to the words used when you were made Ministers of Christ's Church.

The office of Deacon was thus committed to you: 'Take thou authority to execute the office of a Deacon in the Church of God committed unto thee: In the name', etc.

And the priesthood thus:

'Receive the Holy Ghost for the office and work of a Priest in the Church of God, now committed unto thee by the imposition of our hands. Whose sins thou dost forgive, they are forgiven; and whose sins thou dost retain, they are retained. And be thou a faithful dispenser of the Word of God, and of His Holy Sacraments: In the name', etc.

These, I say, were words spoken to us, and received by us, when we were brought nearer to God than at any other time of our lives. I know the grace of ordination is contained in the laying on of hands, not in any form of words; — yet in our own case (as has ever been usual in the Church) words of blessing have accompanied the act. Thus we have confessed before God our belief that through the Bishop who ordained us, we received the Holy Ghost, the power to bind and to lose, to administer the Sacraments, and to preach. Now *how* is he able to give these great gifts? *Whence* is his right? Are these words idle (which would be taking God's name in vain), or do they express merely a wish (which surely is very far below their meaning), or do they not rather indicate that the Speaker is conveying a gift? Surely they can mean nothing short of this. But whence, I ask, his right to do so? Has he any right, except as having received the power from those who consecrated him to be a Bishop? He could not give what he had never received. It is plain then that he but *transmits*; and that the Christian Ministry is a *succession*. And if we trace back the power of ordination from hand to hand, of course we shall come to the Apostles at last. We know we do, as a plain historical fact: and therefore all we, who have been ordained Clergy, in the very form of our ordination acknowledged the doctrine of the Apostolical Succession.

And for the same reason, we must necessarily consider none to be *really* ordained who have not *thus* been ordained. For if ordination is a divine ordinance, it must be necessary; and if it is not a divine ordinance, how dare we use it? Therefore all who use it, all of *us*, must consider it necessary. As well might we pretend the Sacraments are not necessary to Salvation, while we make use of the offices of the Liturgy; for when God appoints means of grace, they are *the* means.

I do not see how any one can escape from this plain view of the subject, except (as I have already hinted) by declaring that the words do not mean all that they say. But only reflect what a most unseemly time for random words is that in which Ministers are set apart for their office. Do we not adopt a Liturgy, *in order* to hinder inconsiderate idle language, and shall we, in the most sacred of all services, write down, subscribe, and use again and again forms of speech, which have not been weighed, and cannot be taken strictly?

Therefore, my dear Brethren, act up to your professions. Let it not be said that you have neglected a gift; for if you have the Spirit of the Apostles on you, surely this *is* a great gift. 'Stir up the gift of God which is in you'. Make much of it. Show your value of it. Keep it before your minds as an honourable badge, far higher than that secular respectability, or cultivation, or polish, or learning, or rank, which gives you a hearing with the many. Tell *them* of your gift. The times will soon drive you to do this, if you mean to be still any thing. But wait not for the times. Do not be compelled, by the world's forsaking you, to recur as if unwillingly to the high source of your authority. Speak out now, before you are forced, both as glorying in your privilege, and to ensure your rightful honour from your people. A notion has gone abroad that they can take away your power. They think they have given and can take it away. They think it lies in the Church property, and they know that they have politically the power to confiscate that property. They have been deluded into a notion that present palpable usefulness, produceable results, acceptableness to your flocks, that these and such-like are the tests of your Divine commission. Enlighten them in this matter. Exalt our Holy Fathers, the Bishops, as the Representatives of the Apostles, and the Angels of the Churches; and magnify your office, as being ordained by them to take part in their Ministry.

But if you will not adopt my view of the subject, which I offer to you, not doubtingly, yet (I hope) respectfully, at all events, choose your side. *To remain neuter much longer will be itself to take a part. Choose* you side; since side you shortly must with one or other party, even though you do nothing. Fear to be of those whose line is decided for them by chance circumstances, and who may perchance find themselves with the enemies of Christ, while they think but to remove themselves from worldly politics. Such abstinence is impossible in troublous times. 'He that is not with Me is against Me, and he that gathereth not with Me scattereth abroad'.

4. *The section on 'seats and pews' from Archdeacon Walter King's instructions to churchwardens, issued in 1841, and found among the records of the then Evangelical parish of Teston* [KAO, P365/8/2]

The arguments of the archdeacon in favour of a reform of church seating arrangements foreshadow the campaign in favour of free and open seating begun by the Cambridge Camden Society, and gradually implemented throughout the second half of the nineteenth century, usually as part of a church restoration programme. Walter King was archdeacon of Rochester 1827–59; the evidence of his clearly stated opinions is a further contradiction of the allegation made by some reformers, and by later commentators, that the Anglican establishment before 1850 was generally lethargic and moribund.

There is no part of your Office, the discharge of which, will require greater prudence and discretion, than that which relates to the appropriating of Pews. The insufficiency of Church room, is a source of frequent and just complaint, and will often place you in a difficult and embarrassing position. It is an evil, which, though the increasing population of the Country tends yearly to aggravate it, may nevertheless be much mitigated by your efforts and arrangement. For the inconvenience often arises as much from bad local management, and illegal encroachments, as from a real deficiency of room. Claims are wont to be set up to Pews, and allowed, under a pretence, which the law would never recognise. Sometimes a few of the principal Inhabitants, to the exclusion or inconvenience of others equally respectable, are allowed to appropriate to themselves all the most conveniently situated seats in a Church. Again allotments of Pews are made, totally disproportionate in size to the wants of those demanding them.

Now it should be understood, that subject to Faculties and prescriptive Rights, by the general law and of common right, all the Pews in the body of a Parish Church, are the common property of the Parishioners; for whose use they are, and who are entitled to be seated by the proper authorities, orderly and conveniently, so as best to provide for the accommodation of all. The Parishioners indeed have a claim, recognised by law, to be seated according to their rank and station. But the higher classes must not be accommodated beyond their real wants, to the exclusion of their poorer neighbours, who are equally entitled to accommodation, though not to the same degree of accommodation, supposing the seats to be not all equally convenient; Inasmuch then as Pews are erected for the use of the Parishioners, whose common property they are, there can be no such thing as *personal* property in Pews; unless indeed by Faculty granted by the Ordinary, or by

Prescription, which presumes a faculty. Over all other than those last mentioned, the Churchwardens exercise the immediate control.

It is however highly proper that the wishes and opinions of the minister should in every instance be solicited and attended to. For as the law entrusts the placing of the Parishioners in Church, and the distribution of seats, to the Bishop, as the most proper Person, by reason of his being charged with the general Cure of souls within his diocese; so it is highly proper, that under similar circumstances, deference and respect should be paid to the suggestions and judgment of the Minister, inasmuch as to him is immediately committed the care of the souls of the Parishioners. You are in fact merely the officers of the Bishop, appointed for the sake of convenience, and the preservation of peace and quiet. And consequently the power you possess is not to be exercised arbitrarily nor capriciously, but with due attention to all reasonable and equitable claims. And should any dereliction of duty, or vexatious interference be suggested and shewn against you, the Ordinary will immediately take cognizance thereof.

On the supposition that the population of your parish requires a strict attention and rigid adherence to the law relative to the distribution of seats, it will be your duty to see that claims are not set up and persisted in, which would debar others from the enjoyment of their just rights. Not that you would be justified in vexatious interference, and unnecessary interruption of a long established holding; still, milder methods of establishing the general right having proved unavailing, it will be your duty to put Persons to the proof of their claims.

Much may often be done by dividing pews; still more by taking down the ancient square pew, and reconstructing it after the modern and more eligible form. And though indeed it be a general and salutary rule, that no alteration in the Church should be undertaken without the sanction of the Ordinary, yet the approval of the Minister and principal Inhabitants having been previously obtained, *small* alterations may be affected without application for a Faculty. Offence is frequently given by the mixing of families in pews. It is a matter of feeling with many to perform their religious duties by the sides of their wives and families. It is a matter of practical benefit, so far as may be to indulge this feeling. Parents in that case are more attentive, as setting an example to their children, who are likely to be and undoubtedly in many instances are benefited by that example. As a matter therefore of feeling and practical advantage, families should be seated together in Church, where this can be done.

5. *Extracts from James Barr's 'Anglican Church Architecture with some remarks upon Ecclesiastical Furniture', 2nd edition, 1843*

James Barr (1810–69) was an architect who dedicated this volume to the Oxford Society for Promoting the Study of Gothic Architecture. The first edition appeared in 1841, and a second, much enlarged, one two years later. The volume was intended to be a practical guide to other architects involved in the restoration of old churches or the building of new ones, and seems to have been very influential. The ideas propounded in it are entirely consistent with the views being put forward by A.W.N. Pugin, the leaders of the Cambridge Camden Society and other ecclesiologists.

The Chancel

The Chancel being that essential portion of the sacred edifice, which is set apart for the most solemn and impressive administration of the Holy Eucharist, should always be designed of spacious and dignified proportions: it may likewise with propriety be very highly embellished, if the painted or sculptured decorations be of a severe and religious character; the east end is sometimes terminated by a semi-circular or polygonal apse.

The Chancel-floor ought to be on a higher level than that of any other part of the building, and should be paved with encaustic tiles covered with appropriate devices; it is also desirable that either the number, or the arrangement of the mullions and tracery of the windows over the Altar, should be symbolical of the Blessed Trinity, the Altar itself being adorned with various sacred and mystical emblems: the Reredos, or Altar-Screen, in like manner, may be very elaborately embellished, the background of the panels being painted or chiselled with diaper-work, or other ornaments. The faldstool which is used for the Litany is frequently placed at the entrance of the Chancel.

The Sedilia, or seats for the Clergymen, were generally in former times arched recesses constructed in the south wall, and on account of their superior elegance, are greatly to be preferred to wooden chairs. A Credence for the reception of the bread and wine previous to their oblation; a Piscina with its basin and drain to carry away the water used for rinsing the chalice; and an Aumbrye, or cupboard, to lock up the sacred vessels, are some of the graceful and convenient appendages of an ancient Chancel, which might be advantageously retained for the service of the Church of England.

The Altar

The Altar is generally elevated on three steps at the east end of the Chancel, and ought to be constructed either of stone or of some costly wood, but the former material is to be preferred on account of its superior beauty and durability; the front and sides may be ornamented with panels and tracery, containing the symbols of the Passion, or other appropriate sculpture. The Altar-cloth which is ordered to be provided is usually of velvet, embroidered with the Holy Name, the Cross, or some religious and mystical emblem.

The chalices and sacred vessels must be of silver or gold, and should be copied from ancient examples, whose forms are more graceful and convenient, and differ materially from those now commonly used. . . . The service books should be bound in the style of the middle ages, the covers being adorned with richly-worked corners and clasps. In many of the Cathedrals and College Chapels, two candlesticks are placed upon the Altar with large wax tapers.

The Pulpit

The Anglican Church does not prescribe any particular situation for the pulpit, but only that it be set in a convenient position within the sacred edifice; it should, however, be placed in the nave, as in former times, either by the side of the chancel-arch or against one of the adjoining pillars. It must on no account be exalted in front of the Altar, since it is enjoined in the Order for the administration of the Holy Communion, that the Priest is to consecrate the elements in the sight of the assembled congregation, and such an arrangement prevents the possibility of this injunction being properly complied with; it likewise compels the Clergyman, when preaching, to turn his back directly on those sacred mysteries which Bishop Heber remarks 'are, or ought to be, in every Church the chief object of a Christian's reverence'.

The Lettern

The Lettern, or Lectern, is a moveable desk, from which the lessons were read in former times, and is retained for the same purpose in many of the Cathedrals and College Chapels. This beautiful remnant of ancient Ecclesiastical furniture is gradually making its reappearance in our Parochial Churches, and ought always to be used when two or more clergymen officiate, otherwise the reading-pew with a double desk is in some ways preferable.

The Reading-Pew

The Reading-Pew should be constructed of oak, ornamented with perforated panels and tracery, but must on no account be made a lofty and prominent erection like a pulpit, since it is not desirable for the Clergyman, when praying, to be exalted above the people more than is necessary for being distinctly heard. It ought to be placed on thenorth or south side of the nave, near the entrance to the chancel, in such a position that the Minister may be enabled to look towards the congregation when making his addresses to them or reading the lessons, and when kneeling at prayers to turn towards the Altar: this practice was followed by the Christians of the early ages, and appears also to be implied by the rubric of the Church of England; nor is it in accordance with the becoming and significant order of her ritual observances that the Priest and people should offer their petitions together to the throne of heaven with their faces turned in opposite directions.

The Seats

Pews, in the modern sense of the word, were not introduced until after the Great Rebellion, and appear to have been far from common before the middle of the eighteenth century: it is much to be regretted that the exclusive and fastidious habits of the present day will not admit of their being entirely discarded, for 'earthly state and vain distinction' are quite out of place in structures where Christians meet together as brethren. The seats ought to be made low, and of sufficient width to admit of persons conveniently kneeling. . . . In the nave the benches must face the east, being arranged on either side of the building, so as to leave a central approach to the chancel not less than five feet wide; those at the upper end of the aisles, or in the transepts of cruciform Churches may be opposite the north and south, but none of the congregation ought, on any account, to sit with their backs towards the Altar.

6. *Extracts from a Kentish pamphlet debate on the doctrine of baptismal regeneration and other matters, 1843* [KAO, Office Library]

The two participants in this debate were the Evangelical perpetual curate of Knockholt, James Sutcliffe, and the non-Evangelical curate of Chelsfield, H. Berkeley Jones. In 1843 Sutcliffe published a pamphlet entitled 'A Letter to the Right Hon. and Right Rev. the Lord Bishop of London, in which the chief doctrinal points of his Lordship's recent charge are proved to be Unscriptural, Tractarian, and Popish'. Jones responded with 'A Reply to the Letter of the Rev. James Sutcliffe, M.A., accusing the Lord Bishop of London of Heresy and Popery'. In his charge Bishop Blomfield had, whilst criticising the more extreme views of the Tractarians acknowledged that 'we are much indebted to those learned pious men, who have forcibly recalled our attention to a branch of duty, too long imperfectly performed', the daily celebration of divine service. Later in his charge, in taking to task those who denied the doctrine of baptismal regeneration, Blomfield had asserted that the view 'that regeneration' does actually take place in baptism, is most undoubtedly the doctrine of the English Church'. Sutcliffe's attack on these views and Jones' defence of them are good local examples of a debate that raged nationally throughout the 1840's, both on the doctrinal questions raised by the Tractarians, and the specific doctrine of baptismal regeneration, which divided Evangelicals from most other Anglicans and which reached its climax in the Gorham Judgement of 1850.

James Sutcliffe
If it be true that 'Popery is the masterpiece of Satan', most unquestionably Tractarianism is the second best of his lying and deceitful works. . Before I proceed to the more immediate object of this letter. . . . I will assume the truth of the following propositions, as being either self-evident or demonstrable by numerous passages of Scripture.

That man, in his natural state, is universally a depraved and sinful creature.

That divine grace is absolutely necessary to change and renew his heart, and, thereby, to make him 'a child of God'.

That the personal experience of this grace is not a fanatical conceit, but a blessed and scriptural reality.

That neither under the Old Testament dispensation nor under that of the Gospel has God ever been pleased to impart his grace to more than a small minority of those who have been favoured with the appointed means of obtaining it.

That the Church of England errs in pronouncing *all* her nominal members to be 'the children of God'.

That in order to his being made 'a child of God', personal conversion is absolutely necessary for every individual without exception.

That the terms regeneration, conversion, renovation, and repentance mean substantially the same thing.

That no unregenerate man can either practically understand or effectually preach the Gospel.

That no young man ought to be ordained to the ministerial office unless he can give to the Bishop a clear, scriptural, and satisfactory account of his conversion and subsequent progress in the divine life.

That every Bishop who does not make personal conversion a *sine qua non* in all candidates for holy orders, is a traitor to the cause of his Divine Master.

That no unconverted man can with any justice or propriety be called a pious man.

That none but converted men ought to be considered as real members of the Church of England.

You affirm that grace is given in baptism. May I ask your Lordship on what passage of Scripture you ground this assertion? . . . take the case either of the Quakers or the Anabaptists. It cannot be denied, except at the expense of truth and common sense, that among the former of these sects are to be found men of sterling, scriptural piety — real and undeniable children of God, who have been 'born of water and of the spirit'; and yet these singular people repudiate the observance of any external sacrament whatever, alleging and believing that the work of religion is wholly and exclusively internal and spiritual . . . I must maintain, without fear of contradiction, that no valid or conclusive argument can ever be drawn from Scripture in favour of baptismal regeneration, for the following reason. In the New Testament there is neither positive example nor precept which sanctions the baptism of infants at all: the instances there mentioned were those of adults, who were capable of answering for themselves, and whose minds, antecedently to the administration of the rite, had undergone a great and fundamental change; so much so, that . . . regeneration took place *before* baptism. It only now remains for me . . . to notice . . . your Lordship's observations upon the manner of performing divine service; such as those upon 'worshipping to the east'; 'placing lights upon the communion table'; 'preaching in a surplice', &c. My Lord, while souls are dropping into hell on every side of us, instead of putting forth any effectual efforts to snatch them from the gulph of eternal ruin, shall we worse than waste our time and energies on such contemptible mummeries as these? . . . I can only say for myself, that if I were to tell the scores of my parishioners, whom I daily see living without one anxious thought about their eternal salvation, that they were regenerated Christians, I should look upon myself as the murderer of their souls.

H. Berkeley Jones
The *foundation* of the righteousness which *procures* the pardon of the sinner, is the righteousness of Christ; the instrument which conveys to him the justifying righteousness of his Redeemer, is the sacrament of baptism; that which sustains it is the sanctifying grace of the Eucharist. This, if I rightly understand his Lordship's Charge, is what he states, and that which the Scripture teaches, and the Anglican Church in all her formularies and creeds inculcates. . . . Some clergymen, to my knowledge, are in the habit of mutilating the baptismal service to suit their own opinions. If it be dishonest in the Tractarians to eat the bread of a Protestant Church, because they defend her doctrines, I think it *much more* dishonest in any minister to continue in her service when he mutilates her offices to suit his own convenience, — and in one of such importance as that for baptism. The views which his Lordship has expressed are those of all the learned Anglican fathers. . . . But, Sir, I

suspect you belong to that school which rejects all interpretation, save that which the Spirit reveals, upon personal prayer, to personal investigation; a school which teaches you to reject all the collateral evidence which may be derived from the writings of learned men. . . . Are you, however, more likely to come to perfect unanimity on any subject contained in Holy Scripture by such a mode? Did Wesley or Whitfield by this means arrive at like conclusions? . . . Surely it had escaped you, that whenever you read the Nicene Creed, you publicly announce your belief 'in one baptism for the remission of sin'. . . . I have now, Sir, waded through your scurrilous and abusive Letter, marked as it is by a want of Christian charity, and that forbearance which you require for yourself at the hands of others. . . . You have attacked the Bishops, — slandered your brethren, — charged that establishment on whose resources you depend, with having transplanted into her 'Protestant formularies' popish dogmas; you have warped the meaning of her Articles, — perverted the language of her Liturgy, — taught her children to disrespect her instructions, . . . You have sought for mercy, that you might attack with impunity; and professed humility, that you might conceal your malignity.

7. *Petition of the inhabitants of East Farleigh to the archbishop of Canterbury respecting the alleged popery of their vicar, Henry Wilberforce, 1844 [KAO, Office Library]*

This was one of the earliest petitions against a Tractarian incumbent, but includes most of the customary complaints made against the Tractarian clergy in the 1840's: intonation of the service, facing east to read prayers, preaching in the surplice, use of lighted candles. Similar petitions to this continued to be drawn up against a substantial number of the Tractarian and ritualist clergy throughout the nineteenth century.

To the Most Reverend Father in God, William Lord Archbishop of Canterbury, Primate of all England; and Metropolitan. The Protest and Petition of the Churchwarden and other inhabitants of East Farleigh, in the county of Kent, in the diocese of Canterbury, members of the Protestant Reformed Church of England as by law established.

It is with unfeigned regret and extreme reluctance your petitioners approach your Grace to allege any complaint against their appointed minister, the Rev. H.W. Wilberforce, whom, as a man, they cannot but highly esteem; but from a strong sense of duty of what they owe to their fellow-parishioners, to their country, and to God, and not from any personal or prejudiced feeling, they feel bound to protest against the following innovations made by him in the services of their parish church, forming, as they believe they do, parts of a plan systematically pursued by a party of the clergy for "unprotestantising" the Reformed Church, and bringing it into conformity again with that of Rome.

I. The departure of the present vicar from the sober but truly devotional manner in which Divine service was performed in the parish church by the late vicar, and the introduction, in its place, of a system of "intoning" the prayers, which is neither saying nor singing, and which, from its unintelligibility to the greater part of the congregation, to say nothing of its irreverence, can never tend to promote the proper ends of Christian worship. Your petitioners have no objection to the chaunting of any part of the service that is the nature of a song, but to chaunt a confession of sin, or a prayer for mercy! (and they have reason to believe it is the vicar's wish to have every part of the service chaunted) appears to them as repugnant to all right feeling as it is destructive of all true devotion. This practice they therefore beg to have discontinued.

II. They have also to complain of the singers being removed from their accustomed place in the gallery into the chancel, as in Popish times, to make way for whom the school children have been removed back into a little private lay-chancel, where they cannot well see or hear. But their chief objection to this is, that it has the effect of depriving the congregation, in a great measure, of their privilege of *common* prayer which was restored to them at the blessed Reformation, which they regard as one of their dearest rights.

III. Your petitioners are humbly of opinion that the vicar's practice of leaving the pulpit, at the conclusion of the sermon on sacrament Sundays, without any blessing, or even a prayer, which gives unnecessary offence to a great part of the congregation, ought to be discontinued, as it cannot be pretended that it is more sanctioned by the Rubric on those Sundays than on others. They cannot but think that this practice has some concealed object, as well as the reading of the word "oblations" in the prayer for the Church Militant, when no oblations are made, in which case the Rubric directs the word to be omitted.

IV. Your petitioners were greatly surprised and grieved to find, that while their new vicar professes to act strictly according to the Prayer-book in all points, the service for the 5th of November, though enjoined by the authority, both of the Church and the State, to be used, especially when, as was the case this year, that day falls on a Sunday, was altogether omitted, and not the slightest reference made in either of the sermons on that day to the two great and happy events which it commemorates.

V. Your petitioners have had their minds offended by the introduction of various novel and superstitious practices by the vicar, which the Rubric no where prescribes, such as turning the back on the people in reading the Creed, frequent bowings, sitting within the communion-rails in the surplice when not reading the prayers, preaching sometimes (which is not a liturgical act) in the surplice, and at the communion-table, and having the Ter Sanctus chaunted while he proceeds to the communion-table on the communion Sundays; and all of which practices appear to your petitioners to indicate a strong inclination to what is Judaical and Popish, and to be calculated to lead people to think that God is to be worshipped by bodily motions rather than in "spirit and in truth".

VI. But what your petitioners most strongly object to is, the restoring of the candlesticks, which had been introduced by the brother of the present vicar, and removed, with the approbation of the parishioners, by the late vicar; and in particular, the burning of lighted candles every Friday evening before a pretended picture of Christ, which was also put up, with a cross over it, by the brother of the present vicar; and which things, when publicly set up in churches, even when not worshipped, one of our homilies declares to be "not things indifferent nor tolerable, but against God's law and commandment". Your petitioners would see no great evil in the mere picture, were not the lighted candles set before it when the service is performed, as it is every Friday evening, not "at the accustomed place", as the Rubric orders, and a sermon delivered, not from the pulpit, and at the proper time, but at the communion-table, and immediately after the second lesson, instead of after the prayers are ended; your petitioners respectfully submit that the whole order of this service is *antirubrical*, and, in particular, that the "setting of lighted candles before any picture" is against the very letter of the injunction of the 2nd year of King Edward the Sixth, which your petitioners suppose to be their authority on which their introduction is grounded, but which, they humbly submit, is no valid authority; because, first, the injunction was only a permission for them "to remain", or to be retained in those churches where they already were and there were never known to be such things in our parish church till they were lately brought in. Secondly, Because "the high altar", on which they were "*suffered* to remain", has long since been done away, both name and thing, from all our churches. Thirdly, Because, the idolatrous purpose for which they were allowed for a time has long been disallowed by subsequent injunctions of the Church. Your petitioners are not so weak as to contend against carved candlesticks, and such like "fond things", for their own sakes, but they object to them as involving certain Romish and idolatrous principles, and that if they are allowed in the church, they will in time give birth in the minds of the people to the same principles in their grossest form of practice, or in the words of the Homily, against peril of idolatry, that "the setting of them up in the place of worshipping" will give occasion to the worshipping of them by drawing the minds of the worshippers to terminate on them. Your petitioners feel bound, therefore, in duty to God, earnestly to entreat that they may be removed.

But, lastly, your petitioners would not express so deep a concern at these innovations, had they not perceived in connexion with them a very different style of preaching to what they have been accustomed, and had not the doctrine which they now hear in the parish church been more in accordance, as it appears to them, with those of the erring Church of Rome, than with those of the Reformed Church of England. It is difficult to single out particular sermons, or passages, where what is erroneous is only now and then amidst much that is good, obliquely insinuated rather than directly asserted, but they would mention in particular a sermon preached on the 23rd of April last, and another on or about the 19th of November, on the sixth chapter of John, in which latter the belief of something tantamount to transubstantiation was strongly urged, and, as it appeared to them, by a method of "handling the word deceitfully", only such passages as seemed to support the literal change of the bread and wine in the Lord's Supper into the body and blood of Christ being quoted by the preacher, and all those which were qualifying or explanatory omitted. All these circumstances taken together, with the introduction of new and very objectionable books into the parochial schools, have excited the deepest feelings of anxiety and alarm in the minds of your petitioners; and this alarm is strengthened by the fear to which an admission of the vicar's "privately" that he kept back his views, has given rise, that further changes are contemplated. Hence they feel imperatively forced upon making this public protest, by the conviction that if these departures from the doctrine and worship of our Church are not timely and firmly checked, more serious evils will follow.

We would not bring these matters before your Grace, had we (the churchwardens) not more than once, first, privately, remonstrated with the vicar upon some of these innovations without effect.

We beg also to state, that before we proceeded to address your Grace, having ascertained that, four-fifths, equally of the higher and lower orders, "or rich and poor", of the parish are decidedly opposed to these innovations, we called a meeting, which we respectfully invited the vicar to attend, but he declined. It was then agreed upon, that a committee of the following five persons (Gabriel Kennard, Jun., and

John Hards, "churchwardens", Edward Post, Thomas Cull, and Thomas Underdown), should draw up an address, to be presented to him *privately*, hoping he would not force upon us the painful alternative of appealing publicly to higher authority; but having waited some time, and found no alteration made, we feel obliged to take this very *painful* step. Our minds are deliberately and firmly made up to resist, by all legitimate means, the introduction of any modified system of Popery in our parish. Yet being very unwilling to leave the church, as some have done, or to do any thing to remedy these things, except through the proper authority, for which we entertain the highest respect; and knowing that the correction of the evils of which we have complained belong properly to your Grace, we feel it to be our duty to lay them now, by this our Petition, before you, "the substance of which was addressed to the vicar". And we do this in the confident persuasion, that as your Grace has publicly declared it as your opinion, that "in the celebration of solemn services the introduction of novelties is much to be deprecated", you will take decided and impartial steps to remove our grounds of complaint, and by your kind paternal interposition, quiet the consciences of a people sincerely attached to the pure Protestant Church, of which you are the Primate.

And your petitioners will ever pray, &c.

8. *Judgement of the Archdeacon of Maidstone rejecting the complaints made against Henry Wilberforce by the inhabitants of East Farleigh, 1844* [KAO, Office Library]

The strong support given to Henry Wilberforce by his archdeacon is very typical of the defence of the early Tractarians by old-fashioned 'high churchmen'. The development of more extreme forms of ritualism, and the appointment of generally less sympathetic bishops, after 1850 meant that those accused of ritual innovations could not necessarily depend on receiving episcopal or archidiaconal support, but even so many of the higher clergy continued to go to considerable lengths to defend zealous parish priests against attacks made on them by their aggrieved parishioners.

I have requested your attendance this day, to announce to you my opinion on certain complaints preferred against your vicar, the Rev. H. Wilberforce, and contained in a memorial addressed to the Archbishop of Canterbury, purporting to be the protest and petition of the church-wardens and other inhabitants of East Farleigh, against certain innovations alleged to have been made by the vicar in the services of their church. These innovations the memorialists describe in very strong terms, as being in furtherance of a plan systematically pursued by a party of the clergy for unprotestantizing the Reformed Church, and bringing it into conformity with the Church of Rome.

Whether such a plan has any existence or not, out of the minds of the memorialists, is not a question on which I am called upon to give any opinion (altogether visionary and groundless as it may seem to me); my business is simply to acquaint you with my opinion as to the manner in which the duty is performed in your church.

As this is the only subject of complaint brought forward by the memorialists in reference to your vicar, I thought the most convenient step for me to take was to visit your church on Sunday morning, and form my judgment, not from the opposing statements which had been laid before the Archbishop, and which are in my possession, but from personal observation on the spot. Among other advantages of this course, it has saved me from the necessity of any discussion. Having been present at the service, I am competent to state what I saw; and I am here to-day solely for the purpose of delivering my judgment on the facts of the case as witnessed by myself, not for the purpose of hearing argument on either side.

The first charge is, that your vicar has introduced 'a system of intoning the prayers', which, 'from its unintelligibility to the greater part of the congregation, to say nothing of its irreverence, can never tend to promote the proper ends of Christian worship'.

And first, with regard to the prayers being read *unintelligibly*. It is painful to meet any statement by what may seem to be a contradiction; but I am bound, in justice to your vicar, to say, that I see no pretence of any kind for this complaint. I have never heard the prayers read with less indistinctness.

With respect to the complaint of intoning the prayers. I perceived that the responses were delivered by the *choir* in the plain, not the musical chaunt, and the effect appeared to me pleasing and devotional. But, with respect to the vicar himself, I was not sensible of any peculiarity in his manner of reading the *prayers*; and in the *versicles* I do not think his manner would have attracted my attention, had it not been particularly awakened. On the whole, however, instead of agreeing with the memorialists in their opinion as to the general effect of the service, it seemed to me to be performed carefully, and with all due reverence. I know of nothing which I should wish to see corrected.

II. The next subject of complaint is the removal of the singers from the gallery into the chancel, 'as in Popish times'. I know not on what authority this is said to have been the custom 'in Popish times'. I perceived no inconvenience or bad effect resulting from the position of the choir; nor, if I had, should I feel myself authorized to direct their removal. It is a matter altogether in the breast of the incumbent and churchwardens, who, in this instance, do not appear to have acted in defiance of any general wish of the congregation in placing the choir where it is; nor can they be expected to move them back, except such a wish should be clearly expressed by the congregation. In my opinion, nothing whatever could be gained by such removal. With respect to the place in which the school children were placed (which is also a complaint under this head), I see no reason why your vicar should not be allowed to consult his judgment, as other clergymen do. If any change for the better can be suggested, I will attend to the subject hereafter, when I come round on my parochial visitation. In their present position they certainly do not incommode others, nor occupy room to the exclusion of those who would desire to occupy their seats.

III. The next complaint against your vicar, as stated by the memorialists, is the practice of leaving the pulpit, at the conclusion of the sermon, on sacrament Sundays, without any blessing or even a prayer. 'This omission', the memorialists are of opinion, 'has some concealed object'. As they do not state the object, I am unable to guess what they exactly mean. I may, however, observe, that the practice of Mr. Wilberforce is strictly conformable with the Rubric, and (so far as the substitution of the prayer for grace, at the end of the Morning Service, in place of the blessing, customary on other Sundays) is observed in all cathedrals, and, I should think, in most parochial churches. On other Sundays the service is not ended with the sermon, and the blessing is therefore reserved until this takes place. The 'unnecessary offence' therefore, has surely not been occasioned by Mr. W.'s practice; or, at least not by any fault of his, but is simply grounded upon the erroneous custom of his predecessor.

IV. The memorialists next proceed to complain of the use of the word 'oblations', when reading the prayer 'for the Church Militant'; and here also they express their belief of 'some concealed object'. As the use of the word is expressly commanded by the Rubric on those days when there is a sacrament, and, as far as my knowledge has extended, always has been used by every clergyman, I must pass over this head of complaint as being founded on some mistake. The memorialists, or whoever drew up the Address to the Archbishop, would appear to exclude not only alms from coming within the definition of oblations, but also the sacred elements before consecration. This is a point often controverted. Of course the congregation may put what meaning they think right upon the word 'oblation', when used by the vicar, when reading the prayer in question; but as he is not at liberty to omit it, and would properly be reproved if he did so, I think I may pass on to the next head of complaint, which is, that on the 5th of November last he omitted to read the service appointed for that day.

As the obligation to read this service does not rest upon the same authority as the other occasional services, but only upon the royal injunction, many persons think that the duty of reading it is not imperative, and some have even thought that it was not legal to do so. I agree with neither of these opinions, but think that Mr. Wilberforce ought to have read the service in due course; but as it is a question which is open to debate, I shall give no advice upon the subject farther than to request Mr. Wilberforce when next the 5th of November occurs on a Sunday, to consult his Diocesan, and to be ruled by his direction, whatever it may be. The omission, right or wrong, was a single act which cannot soon recur, and therefore is not worth debating at present.

V. The fifth complaint is, that 'when reading the Creed the vicar turns his back upon the people', and that he 'makes frequent bowing during the service'; that when 'not preaching he sits within the communion rails in his surplice', and that the 'Ter-sanctus is chaunted when he proceeds to the communion table on sacrament Sunday'.

Now I shall not enquire whether it be, as the memorialists say it is, 'superstitious' to turn towards the altar, when repeating the Apostles' Creed, or (in compliance with the canon) 'to bow at the name of Jesus'. It is sufficient to say, that in neither of these points was the act of your vicar last Sunday, nor his manner, in any respect different from what is done in almost every church in England, so far as my observation has extended. Your vicar turned his back upon those who were behind him when repeating the Apostles' Creed, as he turned his face towards those who were before him: and he bowed at the name of Jesus in that part of the service, but in no other. As to sitting within the communion rail when not preaching, and in his surplice, it is a received custom; to describe it as being superstitious, without saying why, is a proposition which cannot be seriously discussed. So also with respect to the Ter-sanctus being chaunted before the Communion service. It may very likely be a novelty at East Farleigh, but as it is done every Sunday in Canterbury Cathedral and elsewhere, surely it is rash to charge it with superstition. As I did not witness this on the Sunday when I was present, I can only speak of the practice itself, and *that* I cannot think deserving of censure. I do not understand the memorialists to complain of the manner of singing it, but of the thing itself.

VI. The sixth head of complaint is, the restoring of the candlesticks, which, say the memorialists, had been introduced by the brother of the vicar, and removed from the altar-table by the late incumbent, Mr. Lutwidge. This is described as being the foremost offence given by the present vicar, and the one most to be complained of, as the candles are lighted on Friday evenings, and placed, say they, before the picture of Christ: the service, on these occasions, being performed not in the accustomed place, but in the chancel.

The vicar's explanation of this is, that during the time of his brother's incumbency the Friday evening lecture was instituted, and the service performed in the place and in the manner now objected to; that he (the present vicar) resumed the service at the request of certain of his parishioners; that the candles when lighted are placed upon the communion-table, before the picture of Christ, simply for convenience, and with no reference whatever to this last. Such is the substance of the complaint, and the answer to it.

Now as the use of candlesticks in parish churches is not customary, and never had been so in the church of East Farleigh, I cannot pretend to say that I see any reason why it should have been revived in this last, except for some stated convenience. But as candlesticks are placed on the altar, and always have been, in all cathedrals, in college chapels, at the chapels royal, and in the chapel of Lambeth Palace, and probably in other places, I do not feel myself authorized to condemn the use of them as superstitious, or as contrary to the opinion of our Church, nor (supposing this parish were under my jurisdiction as archdeacon) should I feel myself at liberty to leave an order for their removal; because I think your vicar might in such a case demur to my order, as exceeding my just authority. But, as I said before, the introduction of candlesticks is a novelty in the parish of East Farleigh — it seems to give offence to some — and therefore I am willing to do all that I can, which is to ask Mr. Wilberforce to allow them to be removed; not in virtue of my authority (for the reason just now explained), but as a peace offering on his part to those, however few they may be in number, whose prejudices the use of these candlesticks has offended. I am quite willing to put my request into the shape of a personal favour towards myself.

VII. The seventh and last head of complaint is, that the doctrines which the parishioners now hear in their church, 'are more in accordance with those of the erring Church of Rome, than with those of the Reformed Church of England.'

Now charges of this kind may easily be made in cases where they are untrue, and they would be very difficult to substantiate even if they were true. Your vicar strongly and indignantly denies the imputation; which is surely, in absence of positive proof to the contrary, a presumption, at least, of its not being justly founded. But this question I do not mean to enter upon. It is impossible for the memorialists to adduce evidence to prove their allegation, and I am not here to listen to charges which are not supported by evidence. I may, however, observe, that on

Sunday last, the subject of the vicar's sermon having been that of our Lord's Ascension, his discourse was altogether doctrinal; and it is no more than justice to say, that not only did I not hear one word drop from him which could throw a suspicion upon his orthodoxy, but that the course of his argument having led him to touch upon every one of the leading doctrines of the Gospel, he expressed himself in a way which was conclusive as to the soundness of his belief of all the fundamental truths of Christianity: nor do I see any reason to prevent me from believing that the same causes, be they what they may, which have led the memorialists to form, in many instances, a wrong judgment with respect to the acts of your vicar when ministering the service, may also have prevailed upon them to put a wrong construction upon his teaching.

9. *Correspondence between Archbishop Howley, Henry Wilberforce and Gabriel Kennard resulting from the earlier petition of the inhabitants of East Farleigh, 1844–5* [KAO, Office Library]

The five letters reproduced here are a good illustration of the way in which old-fashioned 'high churchmen', like Archbishop Howley, endeavoured to defend the early Tractarians. There is no doubt from this correspondence what his attitudes were to the parties involved, and no doubt also that the attacks on Wilberforce were coordinated by Kennard, the former churchwarden, and based more on personal grudges than on doctrinal considerations.

ARCHBISHOP TO KENNARD, 25 NOVEMBER 1844

With respect to the complaints which you and some other parishioners preferred to me about eight months ago, I made you acquainted with my decision, which was founded on the reports, first of the Rev. Dr. Griffith, and afterwards of the Archdeacon of Maidstone, who, at my request, undertook the inquiry. Two more competent judges, in point of learning, and piety, and knowledge of the particular subjects, could hardly be found, and I see no reason to question the propriety of that decision. I am willing, however, to consider any further complaints with respect to the performance of the Church service, if you will state the charges distinctly and clearly, avoiding generalities, on which no judgment can be formed.

In your letter of the 22nd of this month, you say — '1st, *that the service is performed in a way that is unintelligible and unedifying; 2ndly, that unedifying doctrines are preached from the pulpit — the church being put in the place of Christ, and the sacraments being made of more importance than that inward and spiritual grace of the Holy Spirit of which the sacraments are the outward and visible signs'.*

The first of these charges is expressed in such general terms, that it must be regarded as mere assertion, more especially as it does not concur with the opinion of the Archdeacon of Maidstone, who attended the church for the express purpose of ascertaining in what manner the service was performed.

The second is more specific: it relates to points of so much importance, and is of so grave a character, that it requires to be substantiated by citation of passages, or by reference at least to particular discourses. Indeed, I cannot but think that here there is some misapprehension: it seems to me hardly conceivable that any clergyman should be so extremely absurd as to exalt the church above its Divine Founder, the servants and ministers of Christ above their Lord, or so profoundly ignorant of the nature of a sacrament, which consists of two parts, the outward and visible sign, and the inward and spiritual grace, as to speak of the outward sign as the whole, and even attach to it greater importance than to the inward grace.

You then speak of Mr. Wilberforce's reported intention of erecting crosses — an intention which, could it even be proved to be wrong, not having led to any overt act, would not constitute a legal offence.

You state that Mr. Wilberforce has carried the practice of chaunting the service to a still greater extent than before, so far, indeed, as to deprive the parishioners of the privilege of *common prayer*; but you have not informed me what additional portions of the service are now chaunted, or from what source the anthems which you speak of as having been substituted for hymns are taken.

You complain of the introduction of the word *'blessed'* before the name of the Virgin Mary; but you have not stated whether such is the regular practice of Mr. Wilberforce, or how often it has occurred. The introduction of any word not found in the Creed is wrong; otherwise the application of the term *'blessed'* to the Virgin Mary is justified by the Rubric of the Common Prayer, as well as by the authority of Scripture. (St. Luke, chap. i.)

I have purposely confined myself to those parts of your letter which relate to the performance of Divine service in the church of East Farleigh. Mr. Wilberforce cannot be answerable for what is done or written in other places, or by other persons; nor can I properly notice, on this occasion, that which does not immediately belong to my spiritual jurisdiction.

P.S. — On referring again to your letter, I perceive I have overlooked one of the most serious charges against Mr. Wilberforce — belief in the doctrine of transubstantiation, a doctrine which I have not discovered in any sermon of his that I have seen.

ARCHBISHOP TO KENNARD, 10 DECEMBER 1844

On receipt of your last letter I wrote to Mr. Wilberforce and received his answer some days ago, but I have been prevented by pressing business from acquainting you earlier with the result.

I directed Mr. Wilberforce's attention to the complaint respecting the singing in the church, which appears to me, from his answer, to be conducted without any material variation in the manner , and on the principles which were approved by the Archdeacon of Maidstone; considering that matter therefore as settled by my former judgment, I say nothing more to it.

In respect to the allegations, 'that in the sermons so much is said of the Church and the sacraments, and so little of the merits of our Saviour, and the influences of the Holy Spirit, that the sign is made of greater importance than the thing signified', Mr. Wilberforce affirms that this charge is directly contrary to the truth. The charge of having ever inserted the word 'blessed' before the words, 'Virgin Mary' in the Creed, Mr. Wilberforce solemnly denies. He is certain that he could not unconsciously have made so great a mistake, and he has corroborated his own memory by that of another, who is always present at church. In regard to these charges, the only ones of any importance relating to the Church service (surmises and matters irrelevant being necessarily put out of the question), I am satisfied with Mr. Wilberforce's answers; and I am the less surprised at any mistake that may occur in your statements, as I understand that you have not been at East Farleigh church since the beginning of March last, and consequently cannot speak to the facts you have brought forward from your own knowledge, but must have collected them from common report, or at least from the information of others. With this, as well as the whole of your pro-ceeding from the first, I feel that I have reason to be dissatisfied. On taking offence at your clergyman you quitted the church; you then preferred your complaints to me; I commissioned the Dean of the neighbouring rural deanery to enquire into the circumstances; you excepted to his report; I made further enquiry through the Archdeacon of Maidstone, who, after personal attendance at the church, and communication with different parties, gave in a report, on which my decision was formed. You then come to me, impeaching my judgment, and the Archdeacon's representation on which it was grounded, and preferring fresh charges which you could not to a certainty know to be true.

Allowing you full credit for intentional veracity, I entreat you seriously to consider whether your feelings may not have carried you farther than you will approve on reflection, and whether peace can ever be hoped for, if no individual will cease from disturbance, unless every thing is settled in accordance with his own views. Here our correspondence must end: I should have been justified in bringing it sooner to a close, by your having published my letters without my permission, even before you had received my final reply, at the same time making your own letters the vehicles of censure on the clergyman of your parish, who has been prevented by a sense of propriety, and deference to the opinion of his ordinary, from coming publicly forward in his own defence.

ARCHBISHOP TO WILBERFORCE, 11 DECEMBER 1844

I enclose a copy of my answer to Mr. G. Kennard. Your best plan is to go quietly on, taking care to give no advantage to those who are looking out for points of attack. The public mind is at present in a state of great irritation, and disposed to believe whatever is said against clergymen, more especially such as are supposed, whether truly or not, to be inclined to certain opinions; and these can with difficulty obtain a hearing, even when facts are decidedly in their favour.

In respect to the particular complaints of Mr. G. Kennard, I think the Athanasian Creed, though usually sung in cathedrals, is more properly *said* in country churches. It is left discretional in the Rubric, and is in itself indifferent; but, if not regarded as such by the people, may have the effect, which is always to be avoided, of giving offence. The general improvement of psalmody is very desirable, yet without so much refinement as to prevent the mass of the congregation from joining, and without adding too much to the length of the service.

My experience tells me, that if you persevere in the faithful and diligent discharge of your duties with kindness and gentleness to all, preaching sound Christian doctrine in plain and simple language, not suffering your temper to be ruffled by any provocation, and not appearing over-anxious even in the refutation of calumny, you will in the course of time find the advantage of such forbearance and patience, and, with the blessing of God, will probably see the end of all your troubles.

ARCHBISHOP TO WILBERFORCE, 14 DECEMBER 1844

After giving the most careful attention, as I felt myself bound in justice to you as well as to your accusers to do, to the new charges recently brought against you by Mr. G. Kennard, and receiving your answer, I could come to no other conclusion than that these charges were groundless. This you will already have seen in the copy which I transmitted to you of my last letter to Mr. Kennard.

I have since had a long conversation on the affairs of East Farleigh with the Archdeacon of Maidstone, and his information in regard to particulars has convinced me, not only that I was right in coming to the above-mentioned conclusion, but that both in your communications with your parishioners and in the ordering of the services of the church, your conduct has been such as to give no just cause of offence to any one, and to entitle you to my approbation. The Archdeacon was much pleased with the performance of the service when he visited the church, and is satisfied that it continues to be performed in a proper, impressive, and edifying manner.

KENNARD TO ARCHBISHOP, 6 JANUARY 1845

It is with extreme regret that I once more venture to address your Grace in acknowledgment of your letter of the 10th ult., for the tone and contents of which I was wholly unprepared.

Nothing, to my mind, can be more unsatisfactory than the manner in which your Grace has disposed of the several charges brought against Mr. Wilberforce of preaching unsound doctrines, and of introducing innovations in the mode of conducting Divine service which, from their Romanizing tendency, have had the effect of exciting alarm in the breasts of myself and others who are attached to our Protestant Church.

If Mr. Wilberforce has succeeded in prevailing upon your Grace to believe that the same doctrines are taught, and that the services are conducted in a similar manner to what they were before he came amongst us, and that the divisions which now prevail are referable to an uncalled for opposition to his proceedings, I am not surprised that your Grace should feel dissatisfied with my conduct; but I feel assured if a fair investigation had been instituted into the real merits of the case, it is impossible that your Grace could have come to such a conclusion.

To my own conscience, after serious reflection, I stand acquitted; and in the eyes of the public, if not before your Grace, I have no doubt my proceedings will appear fully justified.

I beg again to assert what Mr. Wilberforce has solemnly denied, that he has inserted the word *'blessed'* several times before the 'Virgin Mary' in the Creed. Your Grace has allowed Mr. Wilberforce to corroborate his testimony on this point by that of another person, but you gave me no opportunity of producing my witnesses (two most respectable persons, who heard it with their own ears) to the truth of what I had stated, although I was prepared to do so in case any proper inquiry was instituted.

Although I have ceased to attend my parish church, and go, at considerable inconvenience, to a neighbouring church, as I myself have informed your Grace more than once, I should not have advanced any thing connected with this painful subject from 'common report', without assuring myself of the truth of my allegations by procuring the testimony of those upon whose information I could place the fullest reliance.

I can fully understand that both your Grace and the Archdeacon of Maidstone were placed in a delicate and difficult position, in consequence of the unusual manner in which the Rural Dean at first prosecuted his enquiry; and to this cause I, with others, mainly attribute it, that no impartial or satisfactory investigation into the grounds of our complaints were subsequently made. We have more than once called your Grace's particular attention to the sermon on the sixth chapter of St. John, as containing, in our opinion, heretical doctrine, and yet we have had no evidence that *that particular* sermon has ever been seen or examined, and to our surprise we observed that your Grace, in your last letter, has passed it over without any notice.

Mr. Wilberforce may affirm that the charges alleged against him are directly contrary to the truth, and your Grace may believe his statements in preference to mine; but I need hardly inform your Grace that the Tractarian party are not distinguished for their strict adherence to truth, where their position requires the contrary, as Mr. Newman, the leader of the sect, acknowledges it as one of their principles, that the Christian 'both thinks and speaks the truth *except* when consideration is necessary; and *then*, as a physician for the good of his patient, he will be *false, or utter a falsehood,* as the sophists say'.

Although, in the course of these my attempts to procure redress, the community at large must have made the painful discovery that ecclesiastical proceedings are not always prosecuted with the same impartiality and regard to justice as those of civil legislation, and that on this occasion there has been a desire evidently manifested to shield the clergyman from censure at the expense of the laity, yet in again addressing your Grace, I feel I have discharged a necessary though painful duty which I owe to myself, to the parishioners of East Farleigh, and to the public at large.

P.S. The following fact will serve to convince your Grace that Mr. Wilberforce's proceedings in our parish are of an unusual character. On the night preceding Christmas-day, Mr. Wilberforce, attended by Mr. Hards, churchwarden, and several men and boys of his newly-formed choir, headed by Mr. Helmore, of her Majesty's choir, St. George's, Windsor, paraded parts of the parish, singing carols; many of them carrying lights, though the moon was high: they were out thus occupied from about eleven o'clock at night till four o'clock on the morning of Christmas-day.

10. *Report on the re-fitting of Christ Church, Kilndown, in 1840–5* [*The Ecclesiologist* iv 91–2)

The new church at Kilndown had been erected as recently as 1839, but was entirely refitted at the expense of A.J. Beresford Hope within a few years of its opening. The contrast between the plain fabric and rich embellishments is paralleled in a similar contrast between the Gothic office books referred to in the description, which still survive, and the communion plate which is completely classical in design. Christ Church, Kilndown, is one of the earliest buildings, not just in Kent but in England, to have been refitted in accordance with the liturgical principles of the Cambridge Camden Society, and has undergone few alterations since that time.

We scarcely know whether we ought to describe the late works at Christ church, Kilndown, as restorations, for the church is quite a modern one. But it was so mean and bad when it passed out of the hands of the first architect, and is now so rich and beautiful in its fittings and decorations, that any account of its present state seems to fall much more appropriately under this head than under that of new churches. The fabrick of the church, except that it is of stone, and of some solidity, is without a redeeming point. A plain oblong room, with low thin roof, broad lancet windows, a mean table for the altar (not even raised on a single step), a clumsy reading-pen and pulpit, and pues, were the chief features of the church when first built. We cannot describe all the steps by which, from what it was, this church has become what it is. The addition of a pierced parapet, of gilt crest to the ridge-line, and of lights to the spire have materially improved the outside; but the inside has undergone the most marvellous change. The pues have been succeeded by uniform open seats in three-inch oak; and without the loss of one seat, a space has been secured sufficient for a moderate chancel, which is now separated from the nave by a glorious rood-screen, exquisitely designed and carved, and coloured and gilt to perfection. The chancel, though on a confined scale, has an ascent of three steps to the sacrarium, where stands the altar, with its credence, piscina, and sedilia. There are stalls for the clergy, seats for the choir, and a noble eagle on the chancel-floor. The choir is lighted by two *crowns*, each carrying six tapers. The floor is covered with encaustic tiles, the walls painted up to the level of the cills with crosses, legends, and diapers; the roof is coloured and gilt; the eastern triplet glows with Munich glass, the jambs being relieved with scrolls; so that with the bright decorations of the rood-screen, and the metallic lustre of the crowns and eagle, and of the gorgeously-bound office-books, a *whole* of colour is produced such as is to be seen, we suppose, in no other English church at the present time. The nave is also partially coloured, and all the windows are of stained glass. We think this church very remarkable, as showing what may be done to produce a religious effect under the most unfavourable circumstances. To any one but the zealous benefactor who has effected this great change (whom the *Ecclesiologist* can scarcely praise lest it should seem to flatter), the task would have appeared nearly hopeless. But his own spirit would seem to have influenced the various artists who have so harmoniously combined to carry out his designs. It is extremely interesting to know that the first steps of the restoration were taken by an Italian architect, Mr. Roos, who has shown that a member of the Academy of S. Luke can appreciate, and successfully imitate the principles of Pointed design. We feel it a duty to mention the other artists who have had a share in this work. Mr. R.C. Carpenter designed the wood-work, screens, and stalls, &c. Mr. Butterfield designed the ornaments, eagle, crowns, &c. Mr. Willement coloured the whole, excepting what Mr. Roos had commenced. Mr. Thomas carved the wood-work. The chancel of Christ church, Kilndown, lighted up for evensong, is a sight which all ecclesiologists ought to see.

11. *Letter from Alexander James Beresford Hope (1820–87), M.P. for Maidstone, to William Ewart Gladstone, 30 December 1846, including a description of the alterations made by the former to Christ Church, Kilndown* [British Library, Add. MSS. 44213, ff.261–6]

The description of the ecclesiological alterations at Kilndown occupies the middle section of what the author labels this 'rambling' letter, and is included to justify his general view of the debate between the extremists and the moderates in the ecclesiological and Tractarian parties. Beresford Hope, like Gladstone, was a moderate but he knew many of the extremists personally and was prepared to defend them against the many attacks made on them by those totally hostile to the Oxford and Cambridge movements. The rest of the letter is devoted to two other significant topics, the difficulties of obtaining a site for the new church of All Saints, Margaret Street, eventually begun in 1850 and completed in 1859, the architect being the Tractarian William Butterfield, and finding suitable ecclesiastical preferment for another Tractarian and contemporary, Benjamin Webb (1819–85). All Saints, Margaret Street, was built to replace the former Margaret Chapel in St. Marylebone, which under the ministry of Frederick Oakeley, from 1839 until he became a Roman Catholic in 1845, had been one of the earliest centres of Tractarian teaching and ritualist innovation in London. Benjamin Webb, co-founder with John Mason Neale of the Cambridge Camden Society, later renamed the Ecclesiological Society, was ordained deacon in 1842 and priest in 1843. He served as curate initially to Archdeacon Thorp, the first president of the Camden Society, at Kemerton in Gloucestershire, and thereafter to William Hodge Mill (1792–1853), rector of Brasted in Kent from 1843 and Regius professor of Hebrew at Cambridge from 1848. He married Mill's daughter in 1847 but had to be content with a curacy to the Tractarian, William Dodsworth, at Christ Church, St. Pancras, until 1851 when Beresford Hope presented him to the perpetual curacy of Sheen in Staffordshire. In 1862 he was appointed, as a result of Gladstone's influence on Palmerston, to the Crown living of St. Andrew, Wells Street, London, and became a prebendary of St. Paul's Cathedral in 1881. Like Beresford Hope, Webb was a moderate in ritual matters, not because of any theological objections to a more advanced ritual, but on the grounds of 'Christian charity, expediency and prudence'. *(DNB)*.

Bedgebury Park
Wednesday, December 30, 1846

My dear Gladstone,

      I wish I could have some more certain good news to tell you about the new church but unhappily matters are again dubious. When the Duke of Portland's price came in it was found enormous besides being clogged with conditions respecting the light of the neighbouring houses. We are in this difficulty that the present coachbuilder seems the man of straw of his predecessor who is still lessee under the Duke of the two houses to the E. of the chapel, and will not sell his lease without one buying that of at least the first of these, a sort of pawnbroker. The Duke's rule is always to regard actual lessees first. The consequence of all these complications was that it turned out that for a moderate area consisting merely of the chapel, coachbuilders and pawnbrokers, we should have to pay (including fee and remainder of leases) £9,000. This seemed preposterous. So we then contemplated building a small chapel on the site of M[argaret] C[hapel] merely (an area of about 70 by 38.8). This would be very small and would face N. and S. but otherwise might be very neatly fitted. I suggested this to the Bishop[1] whom I met at Cambridge at our tercentenary. He did not however approve but rather wished us to postpone, and build a large

---

[1] Charles James Blomfield, Bishop of London, 1828–56.

chapel elsewhere, and not by a small one damage our hopes of that. I then suggested that we should anyhow buy M[argaret] C[hapel] from the government, and spend a moderate sum on better fittings, and to wait patiently for a future site. Richards[2] approved, so did Walker,[3] but found that the Crown might not sell except for a larger church on the same site. Still he had hopes that we might be able to get the coachbuilders without the pawnbrokers. So matters are standing now.

I will not fail giving Walker your message. My wife and I propose all [being] well going to town on Monday to await her confinement. If I can do anything for you then I shall be most happy. Are the hopes of an union of schemes on our ports as impossible as they were last season?

I am very glad that you like my Essay and especially my attempt to discriminate between ceremonies and inward religion. There has as yet been far too little fusion I fear, between those whose [sic] have cared for the outward and the inward movements. Some of the former I fear have been much too merely ceremonialists, and among the latter (especially among those who have now gone over to Rome) a sort of sentimental puritanism was at times cultivated.

You fancy me, I rather think, more merely antiquarian in respect to chancels than I hope I am. I am strongly for *due* length of chancels. What this due length should be may be fairly agitated. I concede at once and willingly that the exigencies of the times, our unchurched towns, the general spread of reading and consequent need of vernacular services put us into a very different position from the middle ages, and that the practical result of that difference is the reduction of the length of the chancel. I repeat it, I think the propriety of worship and ancient symbolism demands chancels, but it does not require them to be just what the chancels of the 14th century were, i.e. varying from ½ to ¼ of the whole length. Our society set off as was natural holding the merely antiquarian view of the case, but we are surely all I think now more rational. When we consider the various apparatus of Catholic worship, and that it must be put somewhere, I think that a tolerably sized chancel will after all be found no greater waste of available space than decency requires, certainly not worse than in many modern churches, which have e.g. a large open space before the altar rails. I should like very much when we meet if you have time to talk to you on the subject. I must give one instance, that of our own church here at Kilndown, a new bad one, which I have been tinkering at. Accordingly to the original plan there were at the east end, an Altar and two huge towers,

[2] William Upton Richards (1811–73), then an assistant in the department of manuscripts at the British Museum, vicar of All Saints, Margaret Street, from 1849.

[3] Possibly Thomas Larkins Walker (d. 1860), architect, pupil of Augustus Charles Pugin, who designed several churches and published various ecclesiological works between 1836 and 1844.

one pulpit, and the other reading and clerk's desks. These having been removed, and a pulpit projecting from the wall, at the expense of *one* sitting having been substituted, space was found for a chancel divided from the nave by a roodscreen and containing on the one side 3 and on the other 2 stalls for clergy (the vestry door making the difference), subsellae under each for 3 boys, and an eagle, and beyond, a sacrarium ascended by 3 steps, and containing an altar, 2 sedilia, a credence, and a piscina. All these are of course greatly crowded, the whole length of the chancel and the sacrarium being a few inches short of 15 feet, and can only therefore be looked upon as a makeshift, still I quote in proof of my τόπος, that the wastefulness (in the room) of Catholic over Protestant arrangement is not near what is supposed. Kilndown formerly could, altar, chairs and all, have only held 3 clergymen and a clerk in the space where 5 clergy and the boys are placed, and by temporary arrangement more on any great occasion might be accommodated, and this was done at the loss of *1* sitting in the nave, and by the projection at the angle of the vestry of a turret staircase to the pulpit.

You will excuse this long rambling description. There is a matter on which I have lately been intending [to write] to you, and wherein if you could do anything you would I can conscientiously say be doing as I conceive a good service to the Church of England. You may possibly know by name the Rev. B. Webb, as secretary of the Ecclesiological Society. He is going to be married to Dr. Mill's daughter, and is anxiously looking out for something if it be merely a curacy. If he can get nothing he is thinking of the colonies. The latter would be a very bad destination for him, as he is a learned clerk and not capable of doing rough hedging and ditching either morally or physically, as it must be done by a colonial priest. He is an excellent man, and one who has entirely risen by his merits, his father being a London tradesman in the city, and St. Paul's school the first nurse of his advancement. He has no worldly means, having just missed a scholarship at Trinity. His ecclesiological knowledge is unquestioned and he is a good theologian and classic, and has no notion of leaving our communion. You will feel strongly how necessary a class of learned clerks is, and how when one is got he should be encouraged. If therefore you could any how be of service to Webb, you would I think be doing our Communion a good turn (I may add that his services to our Society are invaluable). He would be content with a curacy, but his friends of course would be more glad to see him in a living, or an endowed school, or the mastership of an hospital, anything in short permanent. Does Trinity College, Glenalmond (have I got the correct style ?) admit of married tutors or professors? If so and you wanted one I could safely recommend him. You could get testimonials from Dr. Mill and Archdeacon Thorp, etc.

Glynne[4] knows him and likes him. He is a very amiable fellow. I know you will not be angry with me for my frankness and that you will as frankly tell me whether you can or not do anything for him.

Are not the accounts of the destitution in Ireland dreadful? Ought not the English to have some combined scheme for sending them alms?

I have been running on at an unconscionable rate. With united kindest regards and all best Christmas wishes to you and Mrs. Gladstone.

Ever yours sincerely,
A.J.B. Hope

12. *Extracts from the minutes of vestry meetings at Chislehurst in 1848–9 relating to the restoration of the parish church* [KAO, P92/8/4]

Francis Henry Murray saw the restoration of his parish church as his first duty as the new rector of Chislehurst and was able to begin the operation within two years of his appointment in 1846. The architect appointed was Benjamin Ferrey, one of those generally approved of by the ecclesiologists.

9 May 1848
Proposed by Mr. Golding, seconded by Mr. Allen
That the present accommodation in the Parish Church is inadequate to meet the wants of the Parish, and also inconvenient in its arrangement; it is therefore the opinion of this Vestry that immediate measures should be adopted to provide full and more convenient accommodation for the parishioners.

Proposed Revd. F.H. Murray, seconded by Mr. Allen
That it is expedient to rearrange the present seats in the Church in the form which would provide the most additional room with proper accommodation for kneeling.

26 August 1848
Proposed by Mr. Bowden, seconded by Mr. Allen
That the Committee be authorised to apply as soon as possible for a faculty for the enlargement and other alterations of the church recommended in the Report [see doc. 13 below] which has been adopted by this Vestry, and to report to a future Vestry when such Faculty has been obtained.

---

[4] Probably Sir Stephen Glynne (1807–74), M.P. for Flintshire and Gladstone's brother-in-law, a noted ecclesiologist who together with Beresford Hope formed the executive for building All Saints, Margaret Street.

11 January 1849
That this Vestry hereby authorize the Committee to proceed at once to make arrangements for obtaining tenders for the works, and empowers them to commence the works at such time as they shall consider most expedient.

13. *Report of the Committee appointed to consider the alteration and extension of Chislehurst parish church in 1848* [KAO, P92/8/4]

> Most parishes embarking on a major scheme of rebuilding or restoration set up a special committee to oversee the work, negotiate with the architect and contractors, raise the necessary funds, and report progress to meetings of the vestry. This was the case at Chislehurst, where the committee produced a detailed report on the restoration proposals, which was accepted by the vestry.

The Committee appointed to enquire whether it is practicable and desirable to reseat the present area of, and to build a new aisle to, the Parish Church, also to examine the plans, estimates, and specifications which had been prepared for that purpose, have to report to the Vestry.

That they have had an interview with Mr. Ferrey, the architect, and have gone through with him the estimates and specifications; that he states that there can be no difficulty as regards the erection of a new aisle, with perfect safety to the present building, and that he is confident that that work, together with the reseating of the Church, may be contracted for at an expence of £1,180, viz.: £900 for the new aisle, and £280 for the reseating of the old part of the Church, the galleries and chancel excepted.

The Committee have further to report that there will be these additional expenses:–

Architect's commission and journeys, about £70
Expense of faculty 25

£95

      Making a total of £1,275

To meet which estimate there is a list of subscriptions for the new aisle to the amount of £1,051, (exclusive of the legacy of the late Mr. Taggart, the probability of the payment of which appears to be uncertain), and for the reseating, £156 10s.,

      Making a total of . . . . £1,207 10s.

In addition to which they have received promises of support from several parties who have not yet named the exact amount of their subscriptions, but which it is confidently hoped will be amply sufficient to cover the small deficiency, amounting to £67 10s., which still appears. To enable the Vestry, however, to pronounce at once their approval of this very desirable measure, some members of the Committee have pledged themselves to make up the rest of the sum required to meet the Architect's present estimate, should it be necessary, which they trust it will not be.

Under these circumstances the Committee are prepared to recommend the Vestry to adopt the entire plans which have been laid before them, as they consider that they are well adapted to meet the object stated in the resolutions of the Vestry held on the 9th of May last.

The Committee have further to lay before the Vestry some details of the plan proposed by Mr. Ferrey.

With regard to the dimensions of the new pews, and of those proposed to be altered, the Architect recommends, in the plan which he has provided, that they should be *three feet* in height; and the Committee, after examining the models and sections which were prepared and laid before them, having also examined and received accounts from several other churches, recommend that the height of three feet should be adopted in preference to that of three feet four inches (which was before determined upon), as being more likely to secure a due degree of comfort, without injuring the general appearance of the church, or unnecessarily diminishing the accommodation in it.

The other details of the pews recommended are these:–

WIDTH from back to back, two feet ten inches.

SEAT — Height one foot five inches; Width one foot two inches.

LEDGE FOR BOOKS— Width five inches; Height from the floor, two feet six inches, and that there should be a sloping of two inches in the back from the seat upwards.

With respect to the additional accommodation which would be gained by the adoption of the above plans, the statement is as follows:–

The present area of the church, including the chancel,
contains about .... 250 seats
The galleries .... 90 seats
Total .... 340 seats

It should, however, be observed that this is the extreme calculation that can be made, but that the real practical accommodation falls considerably short of this number.

Whereas the old part of the church, including the chancel,
if reseated according to the above plans, would
give .... 284 seats
The new aisle .... 176 seats

The galleries (deducting one proposed to be
   removed) .... 70 seats
                              Total .... 530 seats

From which it appears that a clear gain of about 200 seats may be obtained, together with a much more appropriate and convenient arrangement.

The gallery above alluded to is that commonly called the Singers' Gallery; and the Committee, after maturely considering the question, are of opinion that the general improvement of the church, which would be effected by the removal of this gallery (in which the accommodation is very inconvenient, either for the singers, or for any other members of the congregation) will fully compensate for the loss of the twenty seats which it is calculated to contain. The gallery is at present an obstruction to the light and proper ventilation of the church, both of which would be materially improved by its removal.

There are some other details of the plans, such as the position of the pulpit and reading desk, the width and position of the passages, the arrangement of the seats, &c., which the Committee consider would be best left to the judgment and decision of any Building Committee which may be appointed.

In conclusion, they report that Mr. Ferrey stated that the building of the new aisle and the repairing of the present church, would take a period of about six months; they cannot therefore recommend the Vestry to commence the undertaking before the Spring. But in the meantime they suggest that every preparation should be made for the work, and with this view they now recommend the Vestry formally to adopt the plans which have been laid before them.

Since this was written the hope which was expressed has been realised to a considerable extent, as a further sum of £70 has been received within the last few days, which will now make the amount of subscriptions promised £1,277 10s 0d.; so that it will now stand thus:–

Estimate of expenditure £1,275 0
Subscriptions promised 1,277 10

FRANCIS H. MURRAY, RECTOR,
CHAIRMAN.

14. *Interim report on the restoration of Chislehurst parish church, published in 1850* [*The Ecclesiologist* x 74]

This is a fairly typical report of the type that appeared in *The Ecclesiologist* on restorations in progress. Clearly there was general dissatisfaction that the restoration had not been less conservative, but it was obviously an improvement on the previous liturgical arrangements. *The Ecclesiologist* had very decided views on what was and was not acceptable and stated these views very bluntly.

This church is in the course of enlargement and re-arrangement, under the superintendence of Mr. Ferrey. The original plan comprised a chancel, nave, and north aisle; and, at the west end of the latter, a tower capped with a shingled broach. The whole is of very late Third-Pointed date. A new south aisle is to be built, and the pews, which were as bad as could be, will give way to uniform benches. Most unhappily, it has been thought impossible to dispense with doors to the seats. They will be the greatest blemish in the whole undertaking. We trust that the existing prejudices in their favour will soon be overcome. We may here also express our regret, that the new aisle is to be built in the same debased style as the remainder of the church. The chancel, however, which will probably be re-built, is to be Middle-Pointed. We hope it will be properly arranged and used. For the present, the prayers are still to be said in the nave. The chancel will be raised one step, the sanctuary two more, and the altar will stand on a foot-pace. There is a good screen of Third-Pointed date — which, by an unusual but effective arrangement, being twice returned, separates the chancel from the nave, and encloses, on the south and west sides, a chantry at the end of the north aisle. A new chancel arch, which is to be erected, will, we fear, in some degree, interfere with this peculiarity. Two out of three offensive galleries are to be demolished; the third will, we hope, soon follow. The tablets and monuments with which the chancel is encumbered, will be removed. The roofs will be cleared from their plaister ceilings. The new aisle will have a pretty open porch of wood. The work is not, it will be seen, free from grave faults; but to those who know anything of the parish, it will be a wonder that so much has been done, and in so short a space of time. The estimates for the works were exceeded by the promised subscriptions, some months previous to the commencement of the operations.

15. *Rules of the choir estabished at East Farleigh by the Revd. Henry Wilberforce in 1849, and record of the dispute between members of the choir and his successor as vicar, the Revd. Thomas Watson* [KAO, P142/28]

The surviving choir register for the parish of East Farleigh, covering the years 1849–73, is a unique survival of a contemporary account of an early ritualistic dispute, in the hands of the participants. The issues involved were complex, but the core of the argument was the retention of the type of service favoured by the Tractarian clergy, as opposed to the plainer tradition that had preceded it. The East Farleigh choir was possibly the earliest surpliced choir in Kent, and was certainly one of only a handful of surpliced choirs in England before 1850.

For the Glory of Almighty God and the due celebration of the service of the Church, the Choir of the Parish Church of St. Mary's, East Farleigh, shall consist of the Vicar as Superior, the other clergy of the Parish, and of lay clerks and choristers, united under the following Rules.

1. No person shall be admitted a member except by the consent of all the clerks. Those who desire to join shall first be candidates, and then, if elected, shall be admitted members.
2. Persons in Holy Orders and graduates, or other strangers recommended by the Vicar may be members for the time.
3. Every member shall, to the best of his power, attend the public prayers of the Church on Sundays and Holy days, and a Journal shall be kept in which the names of those who are present at Church, at each Service on Sundays, Christmas Day, Good Friday, and Ascension Day, shall be entered, and also the names of those who attend at each time agreed upon for practice.
4. All monies belonging to the choir shall be kept in the Savings Bank, and a Treasurer shall be elected, who shall pay whatever may be voted by the majority of the Clerks (as for example for rewards to Choristers, for books, for charity or other purposes) and the remainder shall be divided among the lay clerks upon the Feast of the Holy Innocents in each year: each member sharing in proportion to the number of his attendances entered in the journal for the year.
5. A fortnight's notice must be given before any rule can be altered, anything voted, or any member chosen.
6. Every member shall at all times endeavour to live a godly, righteous and sober life as becomes a Christian and especially one who has the high honour of leading the voices of the congregation in the public worship of Almighty God, and in particular to maintain peace and love among ourselves, without reproaches, disputes, or contentions, which come from pride and vain glory; and to be willing to have others thought to be better than himself.

1851 1st Sunday after Christmas

This day the intoning of the Psalms, Responses, and Versicles, singing the Sanctus and Amens and the Morning Anthem were given up as a peace offering to those who object to choral service, at the desire of and on the occasion of the commencement of his duties by the new vicar, the Revd. T. Watson, who this day "read himself in".

Trinity Sunday
This day as a further peace offering to certain persons in the parish the choir involuntarily relinquished the responses to the Commandments and also the afternoon anthem, except on the four great festivals: Advent Sunday, Christmas, Easter, Whitsuntide.

19th Sunday after Trinity (Oct. 26 1851)
In a consequence of a conference between the Rev. Mr. Watson and the quire, from this day the "services" in the afternoon are to be disused and chants used to the canticles. Likewise a Sanctus is to be sung instead of the Sacramental Anthem on Communion days, and an anthem in the afternoon of the first Sunday in each month in addition to the anthems on the Great Festivals. This was Mr. Watson's own arrangement.

[*Note made on 1 February 1852 that choristers wore surplices*]

Saturday Evening February 7 1852
E.P. Hall this day sent in his resignation to the Rev. T. Watson of the office of Honorary Organist, in consequence of his approaching removal to Maidstone, having filled the office gratuitously since August 1849.

Copy of a letter from Mr. E.P. Hall to Henry Roberts, [precentor of the choir],
Sunday Feby 9th 1852
. . . The fact is family arrangements render it necessary that I should return to live at Maidstone. I have introduced Mr. Box in the hope that he would prove a usefull and acceptable successor. I trust I have been of some use to you all during my sojourn here. I cannot help thinking I was sent here in Gods Providence to prevent the total destruction of the Quire and the Choral Service, which I fear would have been the result if you had not had some friend standing in the independent position I did to support you.
There is no question in my mind that if the parish had had to pay for an organist when Mr. Watson first came that they would have stipulated for the entire abolition of all we value in the service, both chanting and anthems. I hope *now* it is placed on a secure footing. . . .

Easter Monday a vestry meeting was held and Mr. Box proposed as Organist but not really appointed till a fortnight after. It was settled at one of these meetings (and that without once having consulted the choir) that no change should take place in the chants to the canticles under a period of 3 months. When this was made known to the Choir they all firmly decided that they could not as a body of singers submit to such usage having given way almost everything for the sake of peace.

A form of resignation was accordingly written out to which each member put his name and it was handed to Mr. Watson, but he feeling sorry to have it done away with handed it to Mr. Ellis desiring him to see what could be done. It was then at the instigation of Mr. Ellis that the choir consented to return under the promise that at the end of this 3 months a vestry meeting should be called and some alteration effected if possible. The same chants to be continued during this 3 months.

The term of our engagement to remain for the three months expired on Sunday June 27th and on Monday the resignation of the whole choir was sent in, there being no likelihood of any alteration in anything to which we considered we had a just claim for indulgence.

The three Sundays following the choir did not sing as usual and only a hymn was sung congregationally.
July 4th   July 11th   July 18th

During this time we went one evening to Mr. Watson's house and he wished to know if we would come back. Mr. H. Roberts [precentor] was not there and consequently it was unanimously resolved that we could answer neither way. This was July 7th. When we left Mr. Watson wanted to know what resolution we came to before Sunday. This was promised. The next evening we went and saw Mr. H. Roberts and talked over circumstances:

July 8th.
Resolved at this meeting that no answer could be returned to the Vicar's question before Sunday, being, as was expressed in the note Mr. Watson received, "too weighty a matter to be decided in so short a time".

Sunday Evening, July 11th 1852
A meeting held at Mr. H. Roberts' for practice. After singing a choice collection of Anthems we again reverted to the question of July 7th Thursday. It was then shewn in this light and understood so by every member present. A form of service was handed to us (Octr. 26th 1851) to which we all assented. At the meeting of the vestry the alteration stated on the preceding leaf was effected. . . . When made known to us a few days after we could but understand that it was an infraction of the treaty of Octr. 26th/51. That, infringement being made we considered ourselves no longer bound to it and so it was determined on that evening to send Mr. Watson a note expressed in the following words
Revd Sir,

We are perfectly willing to retain our places as a choir in the Church provided you will allow us to return to the first alteration made Xmas 1851.
A.M.   Chants to be changed as often as deemed necessary.

Anthem before the Litany on each Sunday instead of the Responses to the Commandments which were retained then but which we are willing to relinquish as we believe you have an objection to them. Psalm or Hymn. Sanctus or Sacramental Anthem once a month.

P.M.   Chants as before said.

Anthem once a month and one on Easter Sunday, Whit Sunday, Trinity Sunday and Advent Sunday.

Amen to be said.

To prevent any mistake we think it better to state that this proposition is made with the understanding that Mr. H. Roberts returns with us. We beg to subscribe ourselves

Most respectfully yours,

The Choir.

The last clause was put in because there [was] an understanding prevalent with Mr. Watson that Mr. H. Roberts did not intend having any thing more to do with it. All agreed there should be no separating.

The following was Mr. Watson's literal answer [*letter pasted into volume*].

Gentlemen,

The arrangement I made with you some months ago, and to which you all agreed, was final.

The present cause of disquietude, arising out of an act of the vestry, I was fully prepared to remove, viz. that the chants should be changed once a month, and also the alteration proposed by Mr. M. Tapfield (to the effect that the sacramental anthem should be sung alternately with the Sanctus) I was quite willing to accede to, as it did not add to the *quantity* of the music, but with any other or further modifications I am unable to comply.

I regret much that I am left in this painful position. I must hereafter endeavour to arrange the singing in the best way I can, and though it will neither in quality or in quantity *from necessity* be equal to what it was before, yet I have the satisfaction of knowing that I have I trust done all in my power and in a Christian spirit to conciliate all parties.

I am gentlemen yours faithfully

Tho[s]. Watson.

Tuesday July 20th. The Choir was kindly entertained at the house of Mr. Ellis, a most sincere friend of the Choir. . . . It was here agreed to leave the arrangement of the whole to Mr. Ellis as several of the parishioners seemed anxious for our return. Through this we did return. The service of Oct[r] 26th/52 [*rectius* 51] to be continued and no further molestation offered or modification made.

Note: This service pattern was still in force when the choir register was discontinued in 1873.

16. *Letter from the Bishop of Rochester to the dean and chapter of his cathedral church commenting on the 'Papal Aggression' of 1850* [KAO, DRc/AZz2/2]

George Murray, bishop of Sodor and Man 1817–27 and of Rochester 1827–60, reputedly the last Anglican bishop to wear his episcopal wig, was typical of the old-fashioned 'high churchmen' who dominated the episcopate before the middle of the nineteenth century. His reaction to the re-establishment of the Roman Catholic hierarchy, and Cardinal Wiseman's inflammatory pastoral letter, in 1850, was actually more restrained than that of many of his episcopal and political contemporaries.

Danbury Palace
Oct. 7th 1850

Very Reverend and dear Brethren,

I beg you will accept my warmest thanks for the kind and much valued expression of your personal regard to me and your attachment to the office I hold in the Church.

I fully concur in the sentiments of just indignation which you entertain towards the Roman Pontiff and his emissaries, for the insults they have offered to our Sovereign, to our National Church, and to the Protestant Faith, and I hope that the general burst of indignation, which has proceeded from all parts of the Kingdom, will have a salutary effect in urging upon the Ministers of the Crown the adoption of such measures as shall vindicate the supremacy of the Queen, and at the same time counteract the present, and any future attempts of the Church of Rome to extend its baneful system of Religion in this Kingdom.

Believe me to remain, with much respect, your faithful friend and servant.

G. Rochester.

17. *Extracts from a Letter to the Parishioners of East Farleigh from their former vicar, the Revd. Henry Wilberforce, dated 10 January 1851* [St. Francis, Maidstone, Parish Archives]

Wilberforce resigned his benefice of East Farleigh in July 1850 and became a Roman Catholic the following September. Like most converts he was violently attacked by many Anglicans, not just Evangelicals but 'high churchmen' as well, and Protestant non-conformists. The letter which he wrote in his defence is a deeply moving account of the religious torments that affected those who could no longer accept that the Church of England, in which they had been nurtured, was a part of the One, Holy, Catholic and Apostolic Church, but merely a schismatical and heretical sect.

My Dear Friends,

I write to wish you good bye, because I could not say what I felt before I left you. I need not tell you how dear you have long been to me, nor how deeply I felt the pain of our separation; and it gives me pleasure, as well as pain, to know that very many of you felt it also. . . .

I know that you have been told that I now no longer believe the things that I used to teach you in Church and in private. This is quite false, as most things are which you hear said about Catholics. I am anxious that you should know it is false, not for my sake, but for your own. It matters little to me that people should think I have been mistaken for many years; but it would be the greatest misery that could happen to you, if you should think that the things I used to teach you are not true and certain; and you might easily think that, it you believed that I, who used to teach them, had myself ceased to believe them. Let me say, then, as solemnly as I can, now that I am leaving you, and when my words are in some respects, like those of a dying man, that they are all true, and all most necessary to be believed. It is quite true that there are other things just as true as these, which I did not know formerly, and which, by the grace of God, I have learned now; and because these other things are not believed or taught by the Protestant Church, I was obliged to leave it; but this does not make the things I used to teach you less true. . . .

Some man may ask me, how I know that the Roman Catholic Church is the true Church of Christ, and that the Church of England is not. My friend, the reasons are a great deal too many and too long for me to tell you half of them. The conviction has come upon me gradually much against my will, and has become more and more deeply fixed in my mind, chiefly by the study of holy Scripture and prayer to God. I think, however, I can easily give you proofs enough to satisfy any man who will allow himself fairly to consider the question; and remember, I beseech you, it is a solemn question. It concerns your own soul; for we have to see whether the Protestant religion is a safe way of salvation for you and me. I am sure it is not, and therefore I leave it, lest I should perish with it, in the great day when the Lord Jesus shall come in the clouds of heaven, to judge the living and the dead, and the world by fire.

Observe, then, in the first place, I know that the Roman Catholic Church, is the only true Church, because she is the only Church that was set up by God Himself. She began 1800 years ago, when our Lord sent out the apostles to teach in His name; and she has gone on ever since. But all other Churches have begun at some time since. For instance, the Established Church is a great deal the oldest Protestant body in this country. But the Established Church began only 300 years ago, when the Catholic Church had already gone on for almost 1550 years; the Church of England is nearly 1550 years younger than the Catholic Church. Before that time there was not one Church-of-England man in the world. All the other sects are much younger than the Church of England. Now, any plain man may see from this very thing, that neither the Church of England nor the Baptists, nor the Independents, nor the Methodists, nor any other sect, can be the true Church of God; for there were no Church-of-England people, no Baptists, no Independents, no Protestants at all in the world 400 years ago. All the Protestant sects have been set up by men who from time to time, thought that they could make a new Church, better than the old Church which had been from the beginning, and more like what they think from Scripture the Church ought to be. For this reason the people who made these sects called themselves *Reformers*. A reformer means a man, who changes things from worse to better. These men were not content with the old Church, which had been from the beginning; they said, "We will make a change; we will have a new Church, which shall be a deal better"; and, indeed, they tried their hands at it. Each one of these reformers, wished everybody else to be content with his own new Church. As soon as he had made his reformation he said, "Now we have had quite change enough: let everything stay just as it is now. We need no more reformation". But other people said, 'No; why should not I make a reformation as well as another? I can make things better than they have made them". For this very reason all the chief reformers were always fighting with each other, because each man wanted his reform-ation and not other people's to be the reformation. And in this way it is that among Protestants one new Church and sect keeps springing up after another even to this very day. It will always be so in all Protestant bodies. The Church-of-England man reformed the Catholic Church, and the Presbyterian reformed the Church of England, and the Independent reformed the Presbyterian, and the Baptist reformed the Independent, and the Quaker reformed the Baptist, and now we have reformed Quakers, till it seems like enough we shall have pretty near as many sects as there are people. But in the middle of all these sects there is one old Church, which has gone on for 1850 years — hundreds of years before any of them were thought of, and before the men who made them were born. This is the Catholic Church. Go back a few hundred years, and all Christians were Catholics; all the new Churches and sects were begun by different men. But the Catholic

Church was begun by Jesus Christ and His Apostles. This shows that it is right, and that they are all wrong. . . .

The Catholic Church is spread over the whole world. This was one of the things promised in the Bible. But all other Churches and sects are found in one country and not in another. For instance, you will never find the Church of England, except where the people are English; whereas the Catholic Church is not only at Rome, but all over the world. This is what the word Catholic means. It means "all over the world". And if you went all over the world, you would find Catholics wherever there are any Christians at all. This was promised to the true Church; and the Roman Catholic Church is the only one that can show its fulfilment.

Another thing is, that the Catholic Church teaches the same things everywhere and at all times. All the Protestant sects are divided among themselves. You never know what a Protestant will believe, and what he will deny, till you have talked with him; and even then, you cannot tell what he will believe, and what he will deny next time you meet him. And this is true, not only of common people, but of learned men and Protestant clergymen, and Protestant bishops. But every Catholic priest in the whole world will give you the very same answer, if you ask him what the truth is. This is something like the truth and it agrees with what St. Paul calls the church — "the pillar and ground of the truth". Oh, how poor a pillar would be the Estabished Church, or any other Protestant body, when we know that there are not two clergymen in the same Church who agree between themselves what the truth is! What is right in one parish is wrong in the next. If there are two clergymen in one parish it is a great chance if they both hold the same doctrine, and when a rector or vicar dies or goes away, it is ten to one his successor alters all he has ever done, and denies most that he has taught. You know you have seen all this yourselves, in your own parish, and in all the parishes round; so that we may truly say, the religion of the Established Church changes as often as the fashions of people's dress or the weather. But Catholics all over the world say the same thing, and in the same words; as St. Paul says Christians ought to do. . . .

You may perhaps think that I must be in some great mistake about this, or else other people and other clergymen would see the truth as well as myself. I should like to explain this to you. The fact is, that a great many besides me have lately seen it, by God's mercy; and have done as I did. Two other clergymen, each possessed of great benefices, gave up their livings and became Catholics almost the same day with me. More than five-and-twenty did the same thing in the course of last year. Multitudes of the poor, in different places, and some noblemen and gentlemen did the same thing. There are few weeks in which we do not hear some new cases of this sort. The present year, I doubt not, will give many more examples than the last. But you may say, "The Protestant religion is three hundred years old; how comes it that we have never heard before these last few years of Protestants becoming Catholics? How is it that there are many whole districts in which there are no Catholics at all, and even in those places where there are Catholic churches, they have almost all been built in the last fifty years? In England it looks like a new religion; though, of course, we know that it is old; that all England was once Catholic; and that many great nations have always been, and still are, Catholic". Now I will explain this, that you may not think what I and others have done in joining the Catholic Church any new fancy. The one thing which kept down the Catholic religion in England for more than two hundred years after the Reformation was sheer persecution. When the Reformation took place, it was not made by the people, but by the King and a few great men, who had the chief power. The King, Henry VIII, wished to marry another wife while his first wife was alive, and the Pope would not let him; and the king, and a great many of the great men wanted to take for themselves the lands which good men had given to maintain the clergy, and monks, and nuns, and the poor, and aged. This made the king and great men Reformers or Protestants. The greatest part of the people was against them; but in those days the laws were made by a few great men; and those who made the Reformation, made the law to take the old Churches from the Catholics who had built them, and to give them to the Protestants, and to force the people to go to the Protestant worship, whether they would or not. Still many Catholics did not go to it; and they were fined, and imprisoned, and cruelly punished. . . .

. . . If I had been vicar of East Farleigh in the reign of Queen Elizabeth, instead of the reign of Queen Victoria (whom may God preserve), and I had openly professed myself a Catholic, I should have been hanged, drawn, and quartered. To avoid this I must have hidden myself, or remained out of England all my life. . . .

Lay these thoughts to heart, dear friends and brethren, and let us pray that, in our several trials and difficulties, we may all have grace from God to "stand firm, quit us like men, be strong". The time is short — the fashion of this world passeth away. Very soon it will be nothing at all to us whether we have been rich or poor, honoured or despised by men, cherished or abandoned by friends. But whether we have indeed been earnest and sincere in striving to know the will of God — whether we have from our hearts prayed to Him to guide and enlighten us to know it — whether we have been ready at all costs to follow it when we knew it — these things will be to us of moment unspeakable, infinite, everlasting. Let this, then, be your prayer: "Give me, Lord, knowledge of Thy will in all things, both small and great. Give me grace to choose, to follow, to do, to love it, at all costs, and simply because it is Thine". Long, my dear friends, has this been my daily prayer; let it be yours, and who can say how soon God by His grace may lead you into that Church into which He has brought me? So be it, by His mercy and grace! And may we all be enabled once and for ever to say and feel with St. Paul, "What things were gain to me, those I counted loss for Christ; yea, doubtless, and I do count all things but loss for the excellency of the knowledge of Christ Jesus my Lord, for whom I have suffered the loss of all things, and do count them but dung, that I may win Christ and be found in Him, not having my own righteousness, which is of the law, but that which is through the faith of Christ, the righteousness which is God by faith".

Commending you very heartily to God, and assuring you that, by His help, you shall never be forgotten in my prayers.

I remain, very dear friends,

Ever yours,

With the most sincere affection,

Henry William Wilberforce.

POSTSCRIPT TO THE FOURTH EDITION, 1854

In revising this edition I have changed the meaning of nothing, but only expressed more plainly some things which had been misunderstood. But having now by the grace and mercy of God been four years in the Church, I desire to add my testimony to that of many others as to the things which I have found there. This letter shows in some measure what I expected. But I thank God I can now say, "It was a true report that I heard in mine own hand", of the glory and blessedness in the Catholic Church. "Mine eyes have seen it and behold the half was not told me; it exceedeth the fame which I had heard". Nay, when I remember the many doubts and misgivings which I felt when I was still a Protestant, and the many fears with which I shrank from joining myself to a system which I hitherto believed to be so corrupt and so horrible, and when I compare these feelings, with the certainty, and peace, and blessedness, which I have found since I had grace to make the venture, it seems to me as if the change I have made can be compared only to the happy death of the just, from which in years gone by they perhaps shrunk with dread, and hardly dared to look forward to it; but to which they for ever look back as their new birth into a state blessed, beyond all that the heart of man can conceive. Oh that every one of my dear friends who are still trembling on the brink of that which looks to them so dark a river, would take courage by our example and risk all upon the faith of the words of Christ. And for myself I need ask nothing else, nor is there anything which others need ask for me beyond the grace of perseverance, that having been sought out by the grace of my Lord and Saviour, and brought into the Church by His mercy, contrary to my own deserts, I may endure unto the end, and through the blood of my Lord and Saviour may lay hold on eternal life. Amen

18. *Letters on Church Matters: XLII Secessions to the Church of Rome, 11 April 1851* [KAO, Office Library]

Alexander James Beresford Hope, then member of Parliament for Maidstone, contributed a series of articles under the general title 'Letters on Church Matters' to the *Morning Post* in 1850–1. All these articles were a defence of 'high church' practice and teaching against its persistent critics, and the one on 'Secessions to the Church of Rome' is a clear enunciation of the view that the Oxford Movement, and even extreme ritualism, did not, contrary to popular belief, actually encourage Anglicans to become Roman Catholics, but rather reduced the number of those contemplating this step by demonstrating that Catholic doctrines and practices had a rightful place within the Anglican system.

I propose addressing a few words to you upon one very painful topic connected with the religious history of our Church for the last seven or eight years, which, as the necessity for it presented itself, I have not been afraid of handling incidentally, but which I have not previously considered in a systematic way. I refer to the various secessions to Rome, of persons whom our Church once regarded as her own, and whose loss, so generally accompanied by some individual incident of a painful nature — as if intended as a special warning to others *not* to do likewise — never fails to be used as a handle by our watchful and ingenious adversaries against the truth of our views; as if the fact of Mr. So and-so being, or not being, in the Church of England could cast a different hue over the pages of the Prayer Book.

I need not expatiate upon the deep feelings of grief with which those whose hearts are in the welfare of the English Church regard the lamentable want of faith which leads so many — forgetful how light even the present suffering is, compared with the days when the Roman Proconsul, and the altar of the false God, or the rack, awaited the believer in the Christian Church — to desert her fold, renounce her orders, and abjure her sacraments, and often, far too often, to place themselves in the conspicuous fore-front of those who heap her with every injurious and bitter-mouthed reproach — men who, while with us, seemed all gentleness and forbearance. This is very grievous, and very grievous is the manner in which the treacherous world deals with it — employing it as an occasion to inflame animosity against those who are feeling a real desolation, which *it* does *not* feel, at the event; accusing those who remain with us of corrupt motives, and at the same time predicating corrupt motives of those who have so often left their worldly all to follow out their unhappy error.

With these facts before us, I think it my duty calmly to view the matter as it stands — to point out why the fact of these secessions having taken place is no argument against the truth of High Church views, or against the fact of these views being the *resumé* of the Prayer Book's teaching — and to give some reasons why the revival of zeal in our Church should have been characterised by such events.

Those who argue in the Tenterden-steeple way do not want any further reasons than they may find in any *Church and State Gazette* to show that the secessions which have occurred demonstrate the falsity of High Churchmen's claims, and justify all the severity and all the injustice with which they have been treated. The more rational observer will feel that common justice requires that, if he were to concede this, he should also demand the acknowledgement that the many lapses, for many years past, of both clergy and laity to Dissent, (of which *we* do not keep a register), are as valid against the opposite party. But I do not intend to try the issue upon a secondary point.

The present position of the Roman and of the Anglican Churches towards each other, and towards the Universal Church, when she was visibly one, is really as follows:–

The "Church of Rome" is composed of many National Churches, and portions of National Churches, which are in communion with the Bishop of Rome, by reason of their acknowledging communion with him as *essential* to Catholic unity — in virtue of his possessing an episcopate derived from a something in the one apostolate of St. Peter which the apostle held over and above, and differing in kind from, that lesser apostolate which he had in common with his brethren, and which has descended to all other bishops. I am making my statement, for brevity's sake, very general — although fully aware that the Gallican Church, for example, recognised of old an apostolate of the collective episcopate of the world, to which the Pope himself must bow; but these opinions, for practical every-day consideration, do not now come into question. The result of this limitation of the Catholic Church to its own body and of its negation of the possibility of outward separation co-existing with intrinsic unity, makes, and has made the Roman Church at all times a working body. It has never failed in fulfilling, in its own way, what it asserts to be the functions of the Universal Church; while, in so doing, it has, in Eastern and in Anglican eyes, built up a vast super-structure as Catholic which is not really so. Still it had the claim of being "The Whole Church" — the form of energizing life.

The "Church of England" — a single National Church, which has, however, by the marvellous multiplication of the Anglo-Saxon race, planted herself in every quarter of the world — at her Reformation rejected those claims of the Roman Church which could not be proved by primitive warrant, and in so doing, she placed herself at once in a primitive and likewise in a confessedly imperfect attitude. In rejecting the seeming completeness of Catholicity comprised in the Roman demands in which she had previously acquiesced, she could only appeal to a completeness of the future — a day still distant in the hands of Omnipotence, when the weak should be strong again, and the withered leaves turn fresh again, and the children of the one Church embrace around their common altars. The Reformed English Church was a Reformed — and, through her reform, an isolated — National Church. The unreformed English Church had been an actual member of what termed itself the whole visible Church. This change, of course, in itself necessitated an appearance of weakness in her action by the side of the great Church of the Continent and of those Englishmen who had not embraced the Reformation. She, by the law of her existence, could not act with plenary power — while their body, by the antagon-istic law of its existence, made, and strove to enforce, that awe-striking claim. Moreover, contemporaneously with our Reformation, came that of other countries, which, in their precipitancy, surrendered what we had preserved — the credentials of identity with the Universal Church. Still, we and they were, politically speaking, on the same side; and many of our soundest and highest divines still cherished the charitable hope that German Protestants would one day crave from us the gift of that which we preserved, and which they had lost — and consequently they involved us in too much moral participation in that denial of revelation which has, unhappily, marked the downward — not up-ward, as they had hoped — course of those unsatisfactory bodies. The dynastic history of England tended to draw closer the bonds of this alliance. The word *Protestant* — used in the land of its invention as the designation of Lutherans exclusively, in distinction to the Reformed or Calvinists — became in England a collective term for any professing Christian of Western Europe who did not belong to the Roman Church — whether he were Anglican, Anabaptist, or Socinian. Again, the term "Catholic", by their constant use of it, and by our carelessness, had become the vernacular for "Roman Catholic"; and so "Catholic" and "Protestant" are, in too many Englishmen's minds, the two fixed antagonisms within the Christian pale. The German and Swiss influences which bore upon England during the Reformation, laid the egg, from which broke out that party to which I have so often alluded — which has ever since existed in our Church without accepting the literal teaching of the Prayer Book, and which is now so very rampant.

The result of all these causes has been that the normal form of corruption in the Reformed English Church has ever been negation of her Catholicity, whether by religious or irreligious persons. The normal form of corruption in the Roman Church, on the other hand, is the allegation of what is un-Catholic as Catholic by the religious, and the cloaking of absolute unbelief under the same designation by the irreligious.

Under these circumstances commenced that great revival of religious truth and earnestness in our Church, of which the first strongly visible signs were shown in 1833. The moving principle of this (by the confession of foe as well as friend) wonderful movement was the Catholicity of the English Church, as shown in her constitution and in the teaching of her Prayer Book. The practical result towards which those who participated in it strove was this — the development through the land, among rich and poor, of those duties of Christian living which the Catholic standard required. The movement went forward, in its own mysterious way — here, possessing the souls of a knot or even a crowd — there touching the heart of some solitary in a moral wilderness. But all who embraced it with earnestness, and with the resolve to act up to its requirements, found themselves engaged in a life which was always one of labour, often of great trouble and anxiety. The love of Church, consolations, and the felt need of the Christian Sacraments, are not things which, when they have once been allowed to lapse into neglect, can be so readily revived. Then came coldness, suspicion — and often rebuke from those to whom natural instinct had taught them to look as fathers. Many of these men were persons of susceptible and tender feelings — many were young men, ignorant of the ways of the world, and of the social laws of impossibilities; and it was no great wonder that they often felt their hearts sink, when they found themselves exposed to reprimand, if not to persecution, for striving to do the work of God in their own Church, as their own Church commanded them. So great a revival, so suddenly spreading over a body so wide as the English Church, left many men necessarily to the influence of private feelings — feelings fed upon in solitude after hard days of ill-requited and harassing labour — or else it congregated similar minds in small knots, only large enough to intensify mutual sorrows.

All the while these men knew that "the head and front of their offending" in the world's eye was their maintenance of the Catholicity of the English Church; and they did not sufficiently consider that a revival must, without a direct miracle, encounter many crosses. This made them often falter in their faith, and exclaim, "Can a church which seems to be fighting against Catholicity really be Catholic?". Present to them, while they indulged in this delusive strain of thought, was always standing that vast corporation which beckoned them on to her — the only Catholic Church, as she assumed herself to be. And, as we know, some have fallen — *some, not many,* if we count how great the phalanx is of those who still are with us.

These falls, most distressing as they are, are clearly, as I have shown, no marks against the Catholicity of our Church. It was, humanly speaking, impossible that such a revival could take place, and yet that all should be right and smooth within it; and as the most pressing trials of churchmen have been from the anti-Catholic side, it was clear that, if unhappily they dreamed the English Church no longer a safe resting-place, they could only rush into the arms of Rome (for Greece was not a tangible reality to any but a travelled few), or else sink into total doubt of all things. But this cannot affect the truths of the eternal Church. If they are written in our Prayer Book, this cannot blot them out — if they are the words of life this cannot change their import. The Church of England is not less or more a branch of the Catholic Church than she was before these secessions. The method of dealing with divine truth must be, to all real men, as changeless as the truth itself, though fallible instruments may shift and falter.

The cause of our losses has been the imperfect exhibition, in our practice, of our Catholic credentials and our Catholic privileges. It would, therefore, have been the part of wise rulers to have laboured all the more earnestly to show that, in spite of the reclamations of Rome, our church contained the saving truth — to have laboured to strengthen her where she was weak, to have fostered everywhere the ripening seed, to have multiplied her indications of Christian love, and charity, and zeal, to have shown a generous and tender confidence to the gentler spirits whom present troubles weighed down, to have urged the rougher and sturdier natures to great deeds of faith. Instead of this, like the old surgeons, they have too often dressed the open wounds with boiling oil. We have seen, for instance, a charge denouncing all and everything about a body of Christians who are told by the hundred of millions, as hopelessly bad and wicked — a sneer dropped during the visitation dinner — some quiet good man who had been spending his life's blood without a doubt of the English Church, treated with marked coldness — some approval of some good scheme withdrawn or modified. Such are the practical methods too often taken to meet a secession; and then persons are surprised that the remedy is so little efficacious.

But still the old truth remains enshrined, as it did before, in the Prayer Book. Still, as before, we protest, as against new German notions, that the Apostolate is needed for the preservation of the truth. Still, as against Rome, we assert that, in the universal Episcopate, and not in the sole chair of St. Peter, the plentitude of this Apostolate is vested.

One more topic must be handled — the assertion that an indulged love of ceremony in our church drives persons over to the Church of Rome. I have seen enough of the state of matters amongst us to be certain that this assertion cannot be substantiated. A craving after more ceremonial, created by over-indulgence amongst us, is I believe, least of all reasons for secession. My proof is one derived from fact. The chief of the early converts have organised a community in England of the Oratorians — and to the Oratorians most recent converts bend their steps. These Oratorians are distinguished by the vehemence with which they resist that species of ceremonialism derived from our older days, and embodied in our Prayer Book, as un-Roman, un-modern, un-suited to the actual Church, "Protestant", and so forth. And yet we are called upon to believe that indulgence in that which creates a craving for more has driven so many over to a system which is noted by its denunciation of that which is supposed to have furnished it with its converts, and that the form of over-gratification is a rejection even of the former more moderate portion. In confirmation of this, I observe that one of the articles of the leading Roman Catholic Magazine for the present month is a favourite topic of that clever periodical — the denunciation of a defence of chancel screens, contained in a High Church review. And yet these chancel screens are held by Lydians to be so fearfully Popish a thing —

Quam parva sapientia mundus regitur!

The last remarks are by way of parenthesis. The facts at which I have hinted in them are deserving of a more careful consideration and a wider notoriety than has been given to them. I must conclude. I have spoken out; and if any one for the future should accuse me of disloyalty to the Church of England, or accuse that system which I advocate, of not being the voice of her trusty sons, and the genuine exponent of her doctrines — first, by anticipation, I deny his charge; and, secondly, I tax him with affinity to the system, not of England, but of Geneva.

19. *Extracts from the journal of the Revd. John Woodruff, curate (1828–34) and vicar (1834–69) of Upchurch* [KAO, P377/28/34]

The journal covers the period 1851–6 and, in addition to the ecclesiastical extracts quoted here, gives an exceptionally valuable insight into the family life of a typical early Victorian country clergyman and contemporary social conditions in a rural parish. Woodruff comments on various political issues, on the state of the weather, on methods of travel, on the treatment of criminals, and provides detailed accounts of excursions to London, to the seaside at Dover, and to other places. He was also a prominent local antiquarian, archaeologist and entymologist and the journal contains several lengthy descriptions of his discoveries and opinions on the discoveries of others.

1851 February 25: Inspected the church [at Alkham], saw a small window which the Vicar had had lately filled with stained glass. A lancet window at the Eastern End of the Southern Isle [*sic*]. The colour good. Subject, our Saviour. The cost moderate. He is to let me know the designer's name, as I have serious thoughts of filling the Eastern windows at Upchurch with stained glass figures.

March 7: Confined to the house . . . with a very bad cold. . . . On this account obliged to put off the duty on Ash Wednesday, intending, had I been well, to perform divine service in the morning. . . . Who would suppose in the present day, that any influence possessed by the Pope could so agitate and disturb the people of this Country. But the appointment of a Cardinal Archbishop of Westminster, together with other Bishops taking titles from Cities in this Kingdom was certainly an insulting step. . . . Altho' the divisions which exist among Protestants are greatly to be lamented, yet no encouragement beyond mere toleration ought to be given to the Roman Catholic Religion. Therefore, I hope, that in spite of the Irish Members, the Ecclesiastical Titles Bill will pass.

Sunday, March 30: After service in the afternoon the farmers came into the Vestry to sign a Petition against the Papal aggression. The petition declared that a more stringent measure was required than the Bill brought in by Lord John Russell, and which has now been read a second time.

March 31: This morning occupied in filling up the Census Paper. . . . This time every one was required to enter their exact age. The Clergy were also favoured with a Paper from the Registrar General's office, which however they were not compelled to pay attention to. I however answered some of the questions, such as the name of the Church, that it was an ancient one, supposed to be built about 1300. How endowed, I passed by. The Tithes being commuted the Registrar General had better get his information from the Tithe Commutation Office. Also the estimated number of persons attending Divine Service on March 30th was requested. There were not so many persons present yesterday as usual, the weather being unsettled. In the morning the congregation amounted, including the schoolchildren, to 78, in the afternoon 147.

April 1: Received a note apparently sent by a Local Preacher, commencing Revd. Brother, and informing me that it was his intention to call meetings in various parishes, and form Committees, for the purpose of resisting Papal aggression. And that a meeting would be held in my Parish in the course of the week to arrange about the Speeches, and that my presence was requested. Of course I considered the assurance of the individual as transgressing the bounds of all propriety. But my indignation was soon appeased by my wife telling me that she was the guilty party. The handwriting was so well disguised, and the sentiments expressed in the letter appeared so natural, that I had not the least suspicion of the quarter from whence it emanated. When the date of this entry is considered, the motive which induced her to send it will be easily discovered.

April 11: Drove over to Chatham, and went . . . to see the carpet worked by the Misses Nicholson for Rochester Cathedral. It is intended to lay round the Communion Table as a pede cloth, and will cover about one third of the dais of the Chancel. The ground is maroon, edged with black, and each alternate square contains a cross or fleur de lis. The border is dark green, relieved with a yellow pattern. They said it had occupied them a year and a half. I am not an advocate for these large carpets for Churches, since, if they get damp, the moth soon destroys them. Handsome marble pavement, or good encaustic tiles, I consider more appropriate.

April 29: Doctor Poore, the Rural Dean, came round on his usual annual expedition to inspect the Churches. . . . I think it a pity that Rural Deans generally have no taste for Church architecture; our Rural Dean's knowledge consists mostly in statistics and legal matters, he brought a basket full of law books with him, but we had no legal question for him to decide. I think this annual visit quite unnecessary, as it only takes up the time of the churchwardens, and we got on very well before Rural Deans were appointed in this Diocese.

September 9: Went to Sittingbourn . . . Archdeacon Harrison preached the sermon, called a Jubilee one, in aid of the Society for the Propagation of the Gospel in Foreign Parts. A large party afterwards met him at the Vicarage. I rather thought of asking him whether he would not give the Clergy an opportunity of signing an address to the Archbishop to let his Grace see how mistaken he was in supposing that not one Clergyman in fifty would deny the validity of the orders of those who had not received episcopal ordination. Not one in fifty, excepting the expectants, would, I am sure, refuse to sign.

1852, February 12: Answered a letter from the Census Office enquiring how many sittings there were in the Parish Church, distinguishing between the free and appropriated. These circulars, I suppose, are forwarded to Country Parishes as well as Town, and tho' applicable to the latter, are not suited to the former. Strictly speaking there are no Pews appropriated in Upchurch, only part of the church has pews in it, but there are quite sufficient for the wants of the Congregation. The population slightly exceeds 400, and the Church could accommodate more than double that number. About five or six years ago the Pews in the Centre Aisle were reconstructed being altered from the large square wooden box to low open seats, so that the Congregation face the Minister. The Pews will hold 216, the seats for the children 60. There is ample accommodation for the Parishioners, for, excepting particular occasions, the average attendance can hardly exceed one third, tho' sometimes one half may be present during Divine Service.

May 11: Drove down to Canterbury to see White at St. Stephen's. . . . Went into the Cathedral to hear the anthem, Mr. Bennett read prayers, who is now in his 87th year, with much earnestness and distinctness. . . . White has improved the situation of his pulpit, and has shifted the screen exactly under the Chancel Arch, which is the right position.

Sunday September 12: [Dover] Went to St. James' in the morning, sat in Mr. Green's pew on the south side of the Communion Table. I think it inconsistent that persons should sit so far up in the chancel, they almost suffocate the Clergyman. I should be an advocate for placing the rails straight across from north to south, and lower down.

November 8: Did the duty yesterday again after two Sundays' absence, being confined to my room for several days with Influenza and a slight attack of asthma. I could get no assistance and the Church was consequently closed on two Sundays. I was sorry for it, as it unsettles the habits of the people. Double duty being now enforced in all parishes the Clergy are fully occupied.

1853 January 12: Distributed 31 gallons of Bread to my poorer neighbours, some of which they received when they came for their clothing club tickets.

March 29, Easter Tuesday: The Archbishop held a Confirmation at Rainham. . . . The present Archbishop (Sumner) follows a different plan from his predecessor (Howley), he delivers an extempore address to the Candidates immediately after the Preface in the Confirmation service, and again when he returns to the reading desk before he pronounces the blessing. Archbishop Howley used to ascend the Pulpit and read an address after the manner of a Sermon. This I liked much better. Luncheon took place at Rainham Vicarage previously, I had the honor, being requested so to do, if I had chosen to consider it such, of sitting next to his Grace.

1854 May 16: South Wharf, Paddington, for the purpose of inspecting some Staffordshire Tiles for repairing the Sunday School Chancel. Selected 750 red and 750 black, 6 inches in diameter, which are to come down in a barge. The day before we had visited Minton's depositary at Blackfriars Bridge, and selected the encaustic tiles which Miss Winthrop has presented to repare the centre Chancel within the Communion Rails. The greater part of which is now boarded over.

May 31: This week the tiles arrived by barge from Paddington to repare the Sunday School Chancel. . . . The traffic of the children had worn out and destroyed the former ancient tiles . . . and I was desirous that common bricks should not be used . . . Sir W. Clay has moved for the abolition of Church-Rates. How long would this fine old country church remain in proper repair if rates were done away with? . . . Dissenters ought not to have everything their own way.

July 18: Mr. Jarvis, stonemason of Chatham, came over with his men to lay down the encaustic tiles within the Communion rail given by Miss Winthrop. . . . The pattern had a very handsome effect, and was designed by the donor. The ground is black and white in alternate squares with red and blue pattern tiles intermixed.

October 12: On the day when the thanksgiving was read for a bountiful harvest the sum of 19s. 2d. was collected which I forwarded to the Kent Opthalmic Institution at Maidstone from whence I had received a circular.

1855 January 10: This day the members of the Upchurch clothing club came for their Tickets. This year 39 had paid in, each was presented at the Vicarage with ½ a gallon of bread . . . the goods were supplied by Mr. Murton of Faversham, and were selected at the School, where the parcels were afterwards sent. The five pounds sent this year by All Soul's College was added to the Club, which with the discount increased their savings by 3s. 7d. each.

20. *Extracts from Francis Murray's 'General Rules for the Guidance of Christian Life'* [Lambeth Palace Library, Longley Papers, vol. 5, ff.121–5]

Murray issued these rules for the benefit of his parishioners in Chislehurst between 1855 and 1865. They are a good example of the pastoral teaching being given by the typical ritualist clergyman in this period.

Spend Sunday holily, cheerfully — it is not to be a gloomy day — spend it in the light of the Resurrection of the Lord; but indulge no noisy mirth or games, and do no unnecessary work upon it. Attend church regularly twice in the day if possible.

Attend some of the Services in the week for the worship of God, especially in Lent, Advent, and on all the Holy Days of the Church.

If you are going on steadily, be regular in receiving the Blessed Sacrament of the Body and Blood of Christ. Have a fixed time for doing so — at first, once in the month and not less, and on all the great festivals; afterwards, you may by degrees come oftener. . . . You may often remain during the Service for worship, though you do not communicate, and it is well to do so rather than to go away. Always communicate early in the morning, if you can, and before you have taken any food.

Every Friday, and fast day during Lent, and any other such days in the Prayer Book, you may observe as follows:–

Do not join in any party of pleasure.

Take less food than you are inclined to take; either by leaving off before you have quite satisfied your hunger, or, if there are two kinds of food before you, by taking that which you like the least.

If you are able, attend some Service in Church, and do some unselfish action for others, But do not make a display of this, or think ill of others who neglect it.

When tempted, make the sign of the Cross, with instant prayer to God for help. Resist manfully, and remember that a sin conquered is a step gained.

If you cannot quiet your own conscience, or desire the special forgiveness of any sins, or require comfort and counsel, go to a priest of God, that you may receive the benefit of absolution, and such spiritual advice as may be needful for you. This may save you years of misery.

21. *Letter from George Edmund Street on the restoration of St. Mary's, Stone-next-Dartford, 24 September 1860* [*The Ecclesiologist* xxi 299–301]

The restoration of Stone church was undertaken by Frederick William Murray, Tractarian rector of Stone 1859–1906, whose brother, Francis Henry Murray, was the ritualist rector of Chislehurst. The architect employed, George Edmund Street, was one of the most distinguished church architects of the period and himself a Tractarian. This letter, published in the *Ecclesiologist*, provides an interesting insight into the principles of Victorian church restoration, which was often unnecessarily destructive. A fuller account of the restoration at Stone, together with a detailed architectural description of the church, was published by Street in *Archaeologia Cantiana* iii 97–134.

Dear Mr. Editor — I gladly avail myself of your office to allow me space for a few lines of appeal to the sympathy of your readers on behalf of the restoration of Stone church.

I hope the merits of the building are so well known to all students of English art, as to make it unnecessary to say much on this head. It is, I think one may almost say, the most perfect and the most beautiful thirteenth century village church of which we can boast. It has been fortunate, too, above most works of the same age, in remaining almost unaltered throughout the Middle Ages: the only additions to the thirteenth century fabric being the steeple at the west end, the western bays of the aisles, and a sixteenth century chantry against the north wall of the chancel. The dimensions of the church are fine, and the care with which the decorations and mouldings are increased in beauty and richness as they approach the chancel is almost unique.

The state of the building before the restoration commenced was this. The nave and aisles were finished inside with flat plaister ceilings, seated with mean pews, and the walls covered with plaister and white-wash. In the chancel the walls had been lowered some five feet, the windows were poor insertions of the fifteenth century, and the only evident relic of the original work was an arcade all round the lower part of the walls, the spandrels of which contain some of the best sculpture of foliage with which I am acquainted. The east window of the north aisle was blocked up by the roof of the Wylshyre chantry. The floor of chancel and nave was level throughout; and the whole internal effect of the church was about as much damaged as it well could be — thoroughly cold and squalid.

We have already effected a vast improvement in the interior, and had we the requisite funds we should be able, without any difficulty, to restore it as nearly as possible to its original state. We have opened the old roof over the nave and aisles (which though not the original roof, is of steep pitch and fair character, dating probably from about A.D. 1500). We have taken down a modern lean-to roof over the north chantry, and substituted a flat roof for it, so as to allow of the restoration of the east window of the north aisle, and the opening of a newly discovered window in the chancel. We have stripped the internal walls of their coat of plaister, and we find that the walls generally are lined very carefully with chalk, on which considerable remains of painting of various dates have been found. These will all be scrup-ulously preserved, and in part (I hope) restored. The lower part of the aisle wall is built roughly with flint, and the chalk lining commences with a course below the stringcourse under the aisle windows, on one portion of which I discovered, I am glad to say, sufficient traces of a running border of thirteenth century foliage to allow of its complete restoration. A border is also carried round the chancel arch, but I doubt whether this is quite so early. On the north aisle wall we find a painting of the Blessed Virgin and our Lord, and two other subjects which I have not yet made out clearly. The clearing off of the plaister disclosed also some architectural features of which no trace had before existed. These are; 1st, two very beautiful quatrefoils (filled in with exquisite foliage, and covered with the original painting) one in either spandrel of the chancel arch. 2nd, a portion of a fine wall arcade in the south aisle. This seems to have been altered very soon after it was originally erected, and we found a portion of a similar arcade built up in one of the chancel walls. 3rd, (and this is the most important discovery) I have found enough of one of the original chancel windows to allow of its complete restoration. There was no trace of any original chancel window; and the only chance of finding one seemed to be in the bay against which the fifteenth century chantry had been built. Here accordingly I cut into the wall, and was rewarded by finding the jambs and monials in their places, and sufficient of the tracery to show clearly the exact character of the whole. The jambs and monials are adorned with detached marble shafts, and the detail is all so rich and so good that I suppose it would be difficult to find a more noble example of thirteenth century work. It is interesting, too, as showing that the same increase of decoration from west to east, which I have noticed in the nave, was continued on into the chancel. The windows at the east of the aisles are very ornate, but the window I have found in the chancel is much more so. The flat roof which we have put on the Wylshyre chantry will allow of this noble window being completely restored and the upper part reglazed. 4th, besides these discoveries, we find great numbers of wrought stones used for filling in the walls where they have been taken down and rebuilt: at present I have looked in vain among them for any remains of the groining. The chancel was intended for groining undoubtedly; and judging by the existence of a flying buttress on the north side, and by the large size of the other buttresses, I can hardly doubt that the groining was erected. Yet, if it was taken down at the time the chancel walls were lowered and the chantry built, one would have expected, and could hardly have failed, to find extensive remains of it. It *may*, however, have been executed in wood; and if so, I should not expect to see any traces of it, for we have found pretty good evidence that there has been a fire in the church which must have destroyed the roof, and would also have destroyed any wooden groin-ing. The traces of fire are seen on the tower walls where the stone is evidently reddened by its action, and in the upper part of the walls we find considerable portions of melted lead, which leaves no doubt that the roofs have been burnt. This fire must have occurred at some time between the erection of the tower and that of the existing roof over the nave — probably circa A.D. 1450 to A.D. 1500 — and in the general "restoration" which it necessitated, I suppose the present chancel windows were inserted, and the old north chancel window half destroyed and then blocked up.

The work now in hand consists of 1st, proper provision for the accommodation of the parishioners (in open seats), the repairing and warming of the church, and the restoration of the ancient vestry on the north of the chancel, for which the funds are already provided; and 2ndly, the restoration, as far as funds will admit, of all the ancient architectural features of the building. This restoration is, as I have shown, no guess work: we have now the most exact information on almost every point as to the original design of the portions which have been destroyed or mutilated, and we are able to guarantee, therefore, a purely conservative restoration. For the accomplishment of this, however, large funds are necessary; and these cannot be raised in the parish itself, where the rector has already contributed a year's income to the work, where the parishioners have given a rate and some subscriptions, and where the architect gives his help as a labour of love. I venture, therefore, to appeal on behalf of this most interesting work to all admirers of thirteenth century art; more especially do I appeal to Kentish ecclesiologists and to the Kent Archaeological Society, and I shall be most glad at any time to explain either here or on the spot the works which we hope to execute. They are briefly, the restoration of the chancel windows, a new chancel roof, the restoration of the groining in wood, and the indurating of all the carved stone work with the composition which has been so successfully applied by Mr. Scott to the similarly decaying stonework at Westminster Abbey.

These are all works as to the propriety of which I suppose there cannot be two opinions, and the completion of which would restore to us the best village church of its date in very nearly all its original beauty.

I need only say that any subscriptions to the work which may be sent to the Rev. F.W. Murray, Stone, near Dartford, or to myself shall be most carefully applied to the works I have described.

I remain,
Yours very faithfully,
George Edmund Street.

22. *Notes on services at Rolvenden during the incumbency of John William Rumsey, vicar 1855–84* [KAO, P308/1/2/1–12]

The twelve volumes of service registers which cover two periods (1862–8 and 1876–83) during this early Tractarian incumbency of a rural parish offer a detailed and fascinating insight into the ways in which a typical 'high churchman' of this period endeavoured to transform his parish. The registers are exceptionally detailed. In addition to the more significant extracts recorded below, they contain a record of the attendance at all services held in the church, notes on various parish events, lists of communicants and the days on which they communicated, a detailed record of church music, accounts of various parish charities (e.g. coal and clothing clubs) and of collections for the various missionary societies.

John William Rumsey was a pioneer Tractarian in a rural setting and he clearly got a very mixed reaction to his innovations. As early as 1859, within a few weeks of their introduction, the noted ecclesiologist, Sir Stephen Glynne, (*Notes on the Churches of Kent*, London 1877, p. 218), had commented on the 'daily services at a quarter past six a.m., and in the evening', even though the church was not at the time fully restored. Indeed it never was completely restored, an indication of the opposition or apathy that Rumsey noted on various occasions, in connection with his introduction of the parish magazine or in trying to ensure adequate preparation for confirmation. Rumsey was not, however, totally unsuccessful. In 1862, in a parish of some 1400 people, he was attracting average congregations of about 200 on Sunday mornings, with about the same in the evening, and a slightly larger congregation averaging about 200–250 in the afternoon. The daily services attracted an average of about fifteen in both the morning and the evening. There was a significant rise in the number of both communion services and communicants; the former were less than monthly in 1862, had increased to 25 a year in 1864–5, to 45 a year in 1866–7, and were weekly, either at 8 a.m. or 12 noon, with additional celebrations on festivals, by 1876.

The outward trappings of Tractarian worship were also clearly in evidence at Rolvenden. By the mid-1860's there were candles on the altar, though probably not lighted, the choir was surpliced and *Hymns Ancient and Modern* had been introduced. The description of the harvest thanksgiving services in 1864 was typical of the Tractarian liturgical standards of that decade; indeed the keeping of the harvest festival with such solemnity, now a hallmark of traditional Anglicanism, was then very much a Tractarian innovation.

2 October 1864: Harvest Thanksgiving (36 communicants)
For the first time Sursum Corda and Sanctus and Gloria in Excelsis

were sung. Choir men and children, communicants and non-communicants, both staying. Organ and choir struck up after I had sung 'Lift up' and 'Glory &c. highest'. Hymn 224 before service. Morning Service was according to general Sunday Evensong use, viz. versicles plain, psalms chanted, Benedicite and Jubilate, Anthem. People waited till after Prayer for Church Militant then they went out without any blessing or organ. Only a pause made. Afternoon Litany choral use only from and after Lord's Prayer inclusive. Evening full choral use. Collection made during hymn after sermon by 6 collectors and brought to the L[ord's] T[able].

Decorations: Floral cross on table. Flowers on it in vases, also minia-ture sheaves of corn. Scrolls on each side of E. window, 'I am the Bread of Life', 'I am the True Vine'. Wreaths of Hops and Ivy pendant from capitals of chancel arch pillars. Font, evergreen and flowers. Reredos, ivy. Nave columns, corn and ivy.

Memorandum of some of the parish acts since 1855 [entered into register for 1866–7]

March 12 1856: I appeared before the Abp of Canterbury to receive his instructions concerning the unbaptized adults in this parish. In the course of the interview, I said 'have I done rightly in refusing to receive fees at baptisms'. He answered, 'You are not only right in refusing, but you would be very wrong in receiving them', and he added 'when a fresh clerk is appointed he should be admonished not to take fees at baptism'. Many children, born since 1855 and not baptized by me, I have since discovered to have been baptized at Tenterden Dissenting Chapels.

Catechizing: When I came, and for the 1st year of my residence, I catechized both schools after afternoon service. In 1857 (Feb.) I changed this for catechizing in church before afternoon service, average 20. Also in 1856 (April) I opened a Bible Class for all ages and I continued this every Friday evening at the National School Room till 1860, average 17.

In 1859 I appointed in lieu of all above mentioned, an hour before afternoon [service] for the teaching of the unlearned and the prepar-ation of the young for confirmation. In 1860 I issued a pastoral letter on this matter, approved and signed by the Bishop, but in vain, it was not in accordance with the 'traditions of men' here, and it languished. Then Advent 1866 I substituted catechizing of the young in service (the catechumens ranged in the choir) for the sermon that they had had for 9 years, and now (Adv. 1867) this institution succeeds and flourishes.

Dec. 1858: Collections 'not at Lord's S[upper]' began to be made from Pew to Pew during the singing of a hymn, or if in the morning, during the reading of the offertory sentences, brought to the altar and offered with Prayer; of course, when in the morning, the Prayer for C[hurch] M[ilitant].

The Daily M. and E. Prayer began (6.15 a.m., 6.15 p.m.) Ash Wednesday 1859, and after trying many hours the present arrangement of 8.30 a.m. and 5.30 or 7.00 p.m. seemed best.

1863–1864: During these two years I issued monthly Erskine Clark's Parochial Magazine. I added a local cover containing much interesting matter, parish records, monthly service calendar, &c. The working classes liked it much but the gentry and farmers would not support it, and after losing about 5 or 6 £ annually I was obliged to give it up. I suppose the cry of 'Romanizing tendency' (a cry only effective on the uneducated, and untaught, and unread, and narrow minded, whether rich or poor) was too powerful.

[1868] *Archbishop Longley deceased Oct. 27 11p.m.*
Bell tolled on the 29th as soon as the news arrived viz. 1 o'clock to 3, minute bell. Altar cloth black super-frontal. Archbishop's chair, black covering. Communicants' rail, black about 12 in. deep. The long foot mat within rails covered. Crape stole. Bell tolled at each service instead of chimes. The above for 2 Sundays, 1st and 8th [November].

Notes on Services 1876–7
Advent: Violet frontal, super altar text. Sacrarium, violet mats and hassocks. Floor carpet taken up. Violet kneelers for communicants. Ambrosian Te Deum, Gregorian chants. Marbeck's Kyrie. Proper Adv. anthems for each Sunday. Sun[day] Even[ing] Adv. lectures.

Lent: Evening Service throughout L[ent] and H[oly] W[eek] at the daily hour 6 p.m. Palm Sunday, altar decorated with 5 stems of pampas grass and 2 bunches of willow.

Easter: Early celeb[ration] choral, breakfast provided at vicarage for choristers after celebration. Noon celebration said. Processional hymns, 107 morning, 291 evening. Full choral service M. and E.

Whitsun Day: Early and late celebrations for the 1st time.

School Fete, Aug. 2: Fine day. Children 219 in premises by 3. Sat down in the Pond hollow by 3.50. Band attended gratis 6.30 to 7.30. Glee singing alternating with band. Band preceded the whole gathering to Church. Over 200 at Evensong.

Sep. 4: Choir to Hastings via Etchingham, 10 men, 12 boys.

23.   *Letters from Lord Richard Cavendish to Archbishop Longley in defence of Francis Murray, 9 and 12 February 1867* [Lambeth Palace Library, Longley Papers, vol. 5, ff.158–61]

Lord Richard Cavendish (1812–73), brother of the seventh Duke of Devonshire, was a parishioner of Chislehurst and one of those prominent in the defence of the Revd. Francis Henry Murray when he was accused of heretical doctrine and liturgical innovations by Lord Sydney. Lord Richard Cavendish had been closely associated with the leaders of the Oxford Movement since the 1840's, and he was a typical example of those members of aristocratic families whose patronage of the ritualist clergy ensured that attempts to prevent them from holding benefices or exercising any public ministry in the Church of England would be unsuccessful.

Buxton Derbyshire
Feb^{ry.} 9 1867

My dear Lord Archbishop,
    I regret very much to hear from Chislehurst that an attempt is being made to get up a memorial to your Grace complaining of 'innovations' having been introduced into the mode of celebrating divine service at the Parish Church. It is now nearly five years since I became a parishioner of Chislehurst, and I can truly affirm that to the best of my belief no alteration has been made in the services with the exception that whereas formerly the surplice was only worn in the pulpit on those Sundays when the H[oly] Communion was administered at midday, now it is worn every Sunday, for the simple reason that a weekly offertory having been established, it would be inconvenient to change it for a black gown.
    I have been obliged to come here for a short time owing to an attack of irregular gout, or I should certainly have now been at Chislehurst, and endeavoured to prevent if possible the peace of the parish from being disturbed, and your Grace from being troubled about the matter. I am reluctant to give your Grace the trouble of reading any letter of mine, but I feel bound, under the circumstances, to bear witness to the anxious desire of the Rector not to offend even unreasonable prejudices on the part of any of his parishioners.
    Your Grace is, I believe, aware that no parish priest can be more devoted to his duties, or perform them in a more exemplary manner than Mr. Murray; and I feel sure that if your Grace could send any person on whose judgement you could rely who should report to your Grace respecting the services at the Parish Church, your Grace would find that there was nothing objectionable in the mode of celebrating them.
    That some of the persons who are trying to get up this memorial to your Grace may be actuated by conscientious motives however mis-

taken they may be, I should be very sorry to deny; but I do not hesitate to express my belief that personal animosity roused by wounded pride and disappointed love of domination, is mainly at the bottom of the proceeding.

I beg to apologize most sincerely to your Grace for thus intruding upon your time, but I feel that, under the circumstances, it is my duty to bear witness to the entire absence (in my belief) of all foundation for the charges brought against one of the most estimable clergymen whom I have ever known.

I have the honor to be my dear Ld. Archbishop with the greatest respect your Grace's most faithful servant.

Richard Cavendish

I ought perhaps to have told your Grace that I have written this letter without anyone else's suggestion or knowledge.

Buxton, Derbyshire
Feb^{ry.} 12 1867

My dear Lord Archbishop

I beg to thank your Grace very heartily for your very kind reply to my letter.

I am not acquainted with the Eucharistic manual to which the Chislehurst memorialists object, and can therefore say nothing about it; but I feel sure that Mr. Murray has no desire to propagate any distinctively Romish doctrine, and for the following reason. On one occasion he made use of language in a sermon which I thought might be so interpreted as to lead ill-informed persons to suppose that he favoured such doctrine on the H[oly] Eucharist, and on my expressing that opinion to him, he said that nothing could be further from his intention, that he thought it possible that his language could be so construed, and that he would take the first opportunity of reverting to the subject, in order to obviate the possibility of such a misconception, and this he accordingly did.

In answer to your Grace's question I beg to say that if I may judge by the overflowing congregations which fill the Church, the great majority of the parishioners are well contented with Mr. Murray's ministrations.

After I had written to your Grace, I thought it right to inform Mr. Murray that I had done so and beg to enclose the answer which I have received from him. I am on excellent terms with the four first memorialists on the list which he gives me. With the two last I am entirely unacquainted. Ld. Sydney I have known all my life and have never received anything but kindness from him, but I cannot conceal from myself that he bears a strong personal grudge against Mr. Murray. In the time of the late Rector, L^d. Sydney's word was law, and he has never been able to reconcile himself to a different state of things. He is moreover not very well informed and has very strong prejudices on the subjects to which the memorial refers. Mr. Berens will always do whatever L^d. Sydney asks him to do. Mr. Edlmann is my landlord, and I entertain a most sincere regard for him. I do not think he would have signed the memorial, if he had been left to himself, but his aunt and sister who live with him, though very excellent persons, are keen religious partisans, and quite as willing to go to a dissenting chapel as to a church. Mr. White is a kind and benevolent person but he belongs to a dissenting family, and is in fact still a dissenter in his opinions and feelings.

I beg again to thank your Grace for your kindness and I remain your faithful servant.

Richard Cavendish

24. *Documents relating to the Folkestone Ritual Case, 1877*

The Revd. C.J. Ridsdale, vicar of St. Peter's, Folkestone, 1868–1923, was the first incumbent, and the only one in Kent, to be prosecuted under the Public Worship Regulation Act of 1874. After his appeal to the Judicial Committee of the Privy Council had failed in 1877, Ridsdale found it difficult to decide whether to accept or defy the judgment. Eventually, after some tactical astuteness by Archbishop Tait, Ridsdale decided to submit, much to the anger and disgust of the extreme ritualists. The following documents are selected from the large number of letters, newspaper editorials and other contemporary comments on the judgement and its aftermath.

(a) Editorial on the Folkestone Ritual Case, *Folkestone Chronicle*, 19 May 1877

Whatever may be the opinion of the result of this case, all who love fairplay must regret the manner in which the prosecution has been promoted. The Rev. C.J. Ridsdale has received considerable sympathy from those opposed to him because they believed the end in this case sought to be obtained, did not justify the means employed. If the three parishioners were really 'aggrieved' parishioners, Mr. Ridsdale would have no ground of complaint. They were not attendants or communicants of his Church, they certainly knew very little about ecclesiastical matters, and they merely consented to be tools in the hands of others.

Mr. Ridsdale could not have greater cause to complain, if three Dissenters, who do not care one half-penny what form his services assume, had been employed to set the law in motion against him. Those so anxious to repress Ritualistic services at St. Peter's, should have waited until they found the real 'three aggrieved' because the spirit of the Public Worship Regulation Act means that those, and those only, who have cause for complaint should be prosecutors. Should there be any future occasion to put in force the Public Worship Regulation Act against Mr. Ridsdale, and we sincerely hope not, we do trust that the three gentlemen who have made themselves so conspicuous will not become a party to the proceedings, but that they will be commenced by those who from association with the Church, are entitled to call themselves 'aggrieved parishioners'.

The judgement must commend itself to moderate men of all schools of thought in the Church of England. . . . We imagine the judgement will fairly please moderate High Churchmen, who, holding advanced views on the subject of the Communion, have yet no intention of revolutionizing the service in question. They have got what they wanted — the Eastward position. Very great importance was attached to this point by men of the stamp of Canon Gregory, Canon Liddon, and Dean Church, whom nobody supposes to be Romanisers. Men of this stamp are not likely to agitate, because they cannot array themselves in gorgeous robes, and whatever agitation does take place will arise from men whose opinion commands the confidence of only a very small section of the Church. Looked upon as a 'compromise' the judgement is eminently satisfactory. It secures for the Church of England that elasticity and liberty which is its glory. No true friend of the Church would ever dream of so narrowing its lines, as to exclude men of the High Church school. The High Church party has been the strength of the Establishment. . . . Ritualism — and by that we mean lighted candles, vestments, incense, and the paraphernalia of the Mass — is the excrescence that has grown out of the High Church revival. . . . It would be premature to speculate on the result of the judgement as affecting St. Peter's Church. We sincerely hope that the Rev. C.J. Ridsdale will see his way to comply with the judgement, especially as the most important point (the Eastward position) has been conceded. If so, the judgement will have the happy effect of restoring peace to the Church of England in Folkestone, which has for some years been disturbed by the most discordant elements, affording . . . an opportunity for political dissent to fling at her its 'flouts, and gibes, and sneers'.

(b)   Editorial on the Folkestone Ritual Case, *Folkestone Chronicle*, 2 June 1877

Last Sunday was a notable day in the history of St. Peter's Church and its Vicar. After a calm and dispassionate hearing of his appeal by the highest Court of this realm, the Judicial Committee of the Privy Council gave their decision against the vestments, and pronounced certain practices in connection with the celebration of the Holy Communion as illegal. Mr. Ridsdale has treated the judgement with contempt by wearing the vestments, and repeating the forbidden practices.

We cannot find the shadow of an excuse for the Vicar of St. Peter's. We have been desirous to do so, because we admire his zeal and earnestness, appreciate the good he has accomplished in his parish, and think that in the manner in which this prosecution was originated he has been hardly dealt with. But Mr. Ridsdale appealed to the Privy Council himself, and when the decision is given against him by that Supreme Court, like a spoilt child he persists in doing all the things he is expressly forbidden not to do. . . . The extreme ritualists not only defy the law, but they will not yield to the persuasion of the Bishops, and after reading Mr. Ridsdale's address of last Sunday, we are constrained to ask, whom will he obey? and the only answer we can make is that he wishes to be a law unto himself. As the State made no such bargain with him when he entered its service, it is only natural that the state will assert its supremacy and public opinion will insist upon this submission.

How different the conduct of the Ritualists from the men who seceded from the Church in 1662, when the Act of Uniformity was passed. We admit that they were originally usurpers in the Church, but when a law was passed which warred against their conscientious convictions, two thousand of the clergy seceded from their livings. We could sympathize with the extreme Ritualists if they resigned their benefices and position. Our sympathy would extend to them if they obeyed the law under protest. . . .. We sincerely regret Mr. Ridsdale's obstinacy, we tell him that he is following bad advice, and that sympathisers with his rebellion amongst the mass of Churchmen are very few.

(c)   Report of services at St. Peter's Church, *Folkestone Chronicle*, 2 June 1877

Considerable interest was excited regarding the services at St. Peter's Church held on Sunday, it having been known that the rev. gentleman would defy the recent judgement. There was an early celebration of the Holy Communion at 7.30 a.m. The vestments, mixed chalice, and two lights upon the altar were used. There were fifty communicants. At 10.30 matins was sung. There was a solemn choral celebration at 11.15 when the vestments, mixed chalice and lights were used as before. . . .

After the evening service a crowded meeting was held in St. Peter's schoolroom to express sympathy with the Rev. C.J. Ridsdale. Mr. Goodspeed occupied the chair. Mr. Birch moved — 'That this meeting, being parishioners and congregation, desires to express the hearty sympathy of the congregation of St. Peter's with Mr. Ridsdale in his present difficult and trying position, and to assure him of its unfaltering determination to support him in his obedience to the plain laws of the church'.

(d) Letter from Archbishop Tait to Ridsdale, 30 May 1877

I understand you believe that there is an obligation on your conscience to follow what you hold to be the literal meaning of the Ornaments Rubric, but that you do not deny that the supposed obligation might be removed by an Act of Convocation of the Province of Canterbury with the proper consents. I gather also from words attributed to you that while Convocation does not so speak, and, indeed, by its silence in its corporate capacity, as consisting of two houses, rather seems to imply that there is no necessity for speaking, and that the Rubrics must be interpreted by such aids as the living executive authorities of the Church can give. I gather, I say, from some of the words attributed to you that you are willing to be guided by me as your bishop. Making full allowances, therefore, for your scruples of conscience, I am quite willing to take upon myself the whole responsibility, as entrusted with the spiritual supervision of the diocese in which you serve. I am ready to use all the authority I possess as diocesan and archbishop to relieve you from any such supposed obligation; and I gladly take upon myself the whole responsibility of directing that you do not wear chasuble and alb at the administration of the Holy Communion, also that you abstain from using lighted candles at such celebration except when they are required for purposes of light; and also that you abstain from mixing water with the wine in the Holy Communion.

I feel confident that, by paying a ready obedience to this my episcopal admonition, you will place yourself in a much more satis-factory position in the sight of the whole Church, that your own people will appreciate your dutiful obedience, and that your labours amongst them will be much more likely to be blessed by Almighty God than you could hope they would be if you acted on your own judgement against the command of the bishop set over you in the Lord.

(e) Letter from Ridsdale to Tait, 6 June 1877

I am heartily obliged by your letter and your kind endeavour to view my position as I view it, i.e. as being under a sacred obligation to act upon the literal meaning of the Ornaments Rubric (whatever the civil penalties of pursuing such a course might be) until a competent Church authority either frees me from the obligation, or interprets the Rubric in some other way. . . . Your Grace kindly offers what doubtless appears a sufficient authority for my acting in the manner you direct: but you will pardon my saying that your words seem to me not altogether free from ambiguity, and in such an important matter I feel there ought to be no opening for misapprehension.

I acknowledge the general dispensing power of a bishop in laws which have (like the Rubrics of the Prayer Book) the authority of the Provincial Synod. If, therefore, your Grace will inform me that your letter of the 30th *ult* was intended to dispense me from the obligation of the Ornaments Rubric, and so from the obligation to use alb and chasuble, lighted candles at Communion time, and the mixed chalice; and further, in view of imminent complications with the State, as your Grace orders me to accept and use such dispensation, I will do so. . . . If your Grace will take into consideration the fact that you have never, throughout these six years during which I have worn the vestments, given me the slightest intimation that you considered I was breaking the law of the Church, you will, I am sure, forgive me for asking you for some assurance that, by your present direction made under my peculiar circumstances, you are (not merely enforcing the late decision of the Privy Council but) delivering your own episcopal judgement to the effect that the Ornaments Rubric does not prescribe the use of alb and chasuble, lighted candles at Holy Communion, and the mixed chalice. and that, therefore my obligation to use these things has been only a supposed one.

On receiving this assurance from your Grace, I will accept your judgement, and, on the principle of canonical obedience, submit my own; and, in so doing, I shall obey your grace as Christ's representative in the government of His flock, so that were the Act under which I have been prosecuted to be repealed tomorrow, or the prosecutors to be pronounced incompetent on account of the venality of at least one of their number, it would not affect my submission to your Grace during your tenure of the see of Canterbury . . . while I submit in the meantime to your Grace, I claim the right . . . to refer myself ultimately to the Convocation of the Province whenever it shall see fit to take the whole matter of the Ornaments Rubric into consideration.

(f)   Letter from Tait to Ridsdale, 7 June 1877

I gather that while you consider yourself as being under a sacred obligation to act upon what you conceive to be the literal meaning of the ornaments rubric in the Prayer Book, you yet acknowledge a general dispensing power in this matter to reside in me as your bishop, and you are ready under such dispensation to abstain from the use of the alb and chasuble, and lighted candles at the time of the Holy Communion, and the mixed chalice. I am quite ready to satisfy your conscience in this matter, and do hereby grant you a complete dispensation from the obligation under which you believe yourself to lie.

(g) Editorial on the archbishop's dispensation, *Folkestone Chronicle*, 16 June 1877

We are afraid that it is too much to hope that quietness and peace will at length be restored to this Parish. The dispensation granted by the Archbishop to Mr. Ridsdale, appears at first sight a clear way out of the difficulty, but it is evident that Mr. Ridsdale has offended many of his own party by the course he has taken, who desire him to carry the principle of resistance to the farthest. Then again Mr. Ridsdale's obedience is conditioned upon the action of Convocation, so that if that body takes no action, he feels himself at liberty to resume the forbidden practices. We cannot view with unmingled satisfaction the action of the Archbishop, for . . . in a certain sense, this dispensation ignores the Court by which Mr. Ridsdale was condemned. However churchmen, will not be too critical if the Archbishop by this means succeeds in maintaining peace. We hope so, but we fear otherwise.

(h) Editorial on the archbishop's dispensation, *Folkestone Express*, 16 June 1877

Three weeks ago Mr. Ridsdale announced to his congregation that he should not obey the judgment of the Privy Council as to certain points which he considered were enjoined upon him by the Ornaments Rubric, and he intimated the possibility of the Bishop granting him a dispensation from the law of the Church. This has come to pass, the Archbishop of Canterbury has done as Mr. Ridsdale evidently wished him to do, and the "droll" circumstance of one of the heads of the Church of England granting a clergyman a dispensation to enable him to obey the law has occurred. It means that Mr. Ridsdale accepts the ruling of the State under protest, and the Archbishop glad, but surprised, to find his unruly minister even so reasonable, jumped at the chance to get out of a difficulty, and lo and behold grants him this dispensation to enable him to overcome his conscientiousness. Mr. Ridsdale did not accept the Archbishop's dispensation at once, but with a suspiciousness which he could hardly have felt with respect to the intention of his Lordship, enquires if the Archbishop's first letter contained a request that he should obey the law, or was really a dispensation from compliance with the Rubric. And on receiving an answer to the effect that his Lordship offered him a dispensation, he only makes use of it because Dr. Tait commands him to do so.

We say nothing with regard to this specimen of the Archbishop's system of management of his clergy, but it does truly seem a most ridiculous state of affairs that he should grant a dispensation for non-compliance with a rubric, which according to the ruling of the Committee of the Privy Council is unlawful.

Be it as it may, it is, however, very satisfactory to find that the services at St. Peter's will for the present be conducted in conformity with the Public Worship Act, and that all the unpleasantness which was likely to arise from the attitude which Mr. Ridsdale took towards the judgment of the Privy Council has been averted by the policy of the Archbishop. But we suppose from the address which Mr. Ridsdale delivered on Sunday night that if Convocation disallows the dispensation he will continue to act in accordance with the Rubric, and consequently defy the law. We hope that Mr. Ridsdale will, during the time which must elapse before Convocation meets, turn his position well over in his mind and if he cannot conscientiously obey the Public Worship Act with regard to the Ornaments Rubric, and other matters, let him vacate his position as a clergyman of the Church of England. If he cannot obey the laws of the body of which he is a member he ought according to all conscience to leave it. But we hope that Mr. Ridsdale will be enabled to continue the good work which he has been carrying on and is still effecting in St. Peter's district. We admire and like Mr. Ridsdale for his conduct as a clergyman, but we object to him putting himself in an attitude of defiance to the laws of the Church of England.

(i) Minutes of the June Chapter of the Society of the Holy Cross, 1877

Motion (carried): 'That in view of the possibility of Brethren being placed in a similar position to Br. Ridsdale, the subject of Dispensation, especially in its bearing on the Ridsdale case, be referred to the Canon Law Committee, with a request that they will report thereupon, and in particular with respect to the following questions: (i) whether a Dispensation is of any value which avowedly does not recognise the obligation from which it professes to dispense? (ii) whether Bishops have the power to dispense, except in cases of extreme necessity, from the ordination vow, or the Law of the Church? (iii) whether it is advisable for the Brethren of the Society to act upon such a Dispensation?'

25. *Copy of a letter from Canon Edward Hoare to the Ecclesiastical Commission objecting to the establishment of the new parish of St. Barnabas, Tunbridge Wells, and to its proposed patronage, 3 January 1881* [KAO, P371L/28/10]

Canon Edward Hoare was incumbent of Holy Trinity, Tunbridge Wells, from 1853 until 1894, and rural dean of Malling. He was largely responsible for establishing a network of strongly

Evangelical churches in the town, and occupied a position of political and social dominance comparable to that held by Francis Close at Cheltenham between 1826 and 1856. Like Close, Hoare was a vigorous controversialist and vociferous opponent of both Roman Catholicism and Anglican ritualism. This letter, however, failed to frustrate the establishment of the new parish of St. Barnabas which, after the return of St. James' to the Evangelical fold, became the lone bastion of Anglo-Catholicism in Tunbridge Wells.

. . . I object still more strongly to the particular division [of St. James' parish] respecting which I am requested to give an opinion. The boundary line proposed separates the greater part of the poor from the rich of St. James's parish. I consider that at least four fifths of the poor of St. James' parish would be assigned to St. Barnabas, and *not one* individual of the rich; I do not believe that there is a house in the proposed district in which a domestic servant is kept;* so that if the scheme is carried out there will be a large poor district utterly unable to maintain its own institutions, and a large rich parish, the parishioners of which will be relieved from almost all parochial responsibility towards their poor neighbours. I consider that this arrangement would be so injurious to both classes that I cannot believe the Commission would ever have entertained the proposal, if they had been aware of the facts.

I strongly object to the assignment of the patronage of the Warden, Council and Scholars of Keble College. I can scarcely imagine a body of men less fitted for the appointment of a parochial clergyman; and the only motive that I can imagine for such an arrangement is the desire to perpetuate the system of doctrine and ritual at present adopted in St. James. That system has driven away from their parish church so large a proportion of the loyal churchmen of the parish, that, notwithstanding the population, the wealthy, and the Christian liberality, to be found in St. James' parish, the Ecclesiastical Commissioners have actually considered it necessary to supplement the income of the vicar by an annual grant in order to make it up to £300 a year; and it appears to me a most cruel thing that the poor of the parish, by whom the system is disliked quite as much as by the rich, should have their wishes and convictions sacrificed in order that it may be perpetuated amongst them.

This sentence, in the original draft, was deleted from the final text.

26. *Extracts from the inventory of St. Nicholas' Church, Chislehurst, compiled during Eastertide 1887* [KAO, P92/6/1]

The inventory is typical of that for any ritualist parish in the late nineteenth century; it would however appear that linen chasubles were still in use in 1887 but that they had been completely replaced by coloured ones before 1902. The large number of candlesticks on the altar and in the sanctuary is also typical. If all had been lighted, as they would have been on major festivals, there would have been forty lighted candles on the altar, a further twenty elsewhere in the sanctuary and even fourteen on top of the chancel screen.

The oak altar with stone slab in the centre
One silver gilt jewelled chalice
Two silver gilt patens, one of them with enamelled cross
One pyx for sick communion
One brass desk for the altar
Altar frontals: one set of white silk damask embroidered including frontal, superfrontal; one set of red velvet including frontal, superfrontal and credence cloth; one set of green silk damask including frontal, superfrontal and credence cloth; one set of violet silk embroidered including frontal, superfrontal and woollen credence cloth; one set of black cloth, including frontal (without superfrontal), black hangings to cover reredos and retable, and a credence cloth
One pair of white dossals, embroidered
One pair of red dossals, (red and gold)
On pair of violet dossals
One pair of black dossals
Two small candlesticks on the credence
On the retable: two large brass candlesticks for the Eucharist lights; one pair of seven-branched candlesticks; eight candlesticks, each having 3 branches
Seven brass vases
Two standard coronas with nine lights each
Two pieces of lace for the altar
Vestments: two linen chasubles; one white silk chasuble; one violet chasuble of silk; seven plain albes; six linen amices; two girdles; one eucharistic stole, cloth of gold, two do. white silk, two do. red silk, two do. green silk, two do. violet silk; one maniple, cloth of gold, two do. white silk, two do. red silk, one do. green silk, two do. violet silk.
Two white silk veils, embroidered, one of them having a crown of small pearls; two white burses, embroidered
One white veil, corded silk, with raised work

One cloth of gold veil; one cloth of gold burse
One red veil and burse, corded silk, with raised embroidery
One smaller red veil, embroidered
One green silk damask veil and burse, embroidered
One smaller green veil (corded silk)
One violet veil, corded silk, embroidered, one burse to match
One violet veil of velvet, with burse
One black velvet veil and burse
Four white silk stoles, embroidered
Two white silk stoles, plainer
Five red silk stoles, embroidered
Four green silk stoles, embroidered
Six violet silk stoles, embroidered
Two black velvet stoles
Three black silk stoles
One ebony and brass processional cross
Two hanging coronas (4 lights each) and chains
Four brass sconces on the screen, two of them for 4 and two for 3 lights
Two violet funeral palls
One white damask funeral pall
Two white cashmere funeral palls worked with silk
One processional banner
Eight hanging banners of needlework

[*Supplementary inventory of vestments dated December 1902*]

Frontals
1 best white frontal and superfrontal figured and jewelled
1 white damask embroidered altar frontal and superfrontal used since
    1849
1 green damask embroidered altar frontal and superfrontal presented
    1898
1 green damask embroidered altar frontal and superfrontal used
    previous to that date
1 red velvet frontal and superfrontal
1 violet silk frontal and superfrontal
1 black cloth frontal, no superfrontal and unmounted

Faldstool and pulpit hangings
1 white damask faldstool and pulpit hanging
1 white cloth ditto
1 green damask 1898
1 green damask in use before that date

1 red damask embroidered with lilies
1 red cloth faldstool hanging, 1 red velvet pulpit hanging
1 violet silk faldstool and pulpit hanging
1 black cloth   ditto

Veils and Burses
1 best white veil and burse (jewelled)
1 cloth of gold   ditto
2 white silk   ditto
1 green silk   ditto
1 green silk   ditto (old)
1 red silk   ditto
1 red silk   ditto (old)
1 violet silk   ditto
1 black silk   ditto
1 black velvet veil and burse

Chasubles
1 white damask embroidered with cloth of gold cross
1 white silk
1 green silk
1 red silk
1 violet silk (new)
1 black silk

Eucharistic stoles and maniples

2 cloth of gold	3 red silk
2 white silk	2 violet silk
3 green silk	1 black silk

2 amices with collars embroidered with gold

1 baptismal stole (violet and white)

Stoles for Mattins: 4 white silk, 4 green silk, 4 red silk, 3 violet silk, 4 black silk, 2 black velvet.

27. *Appeal for funds to build a permanent 'free' Church of England chapel in Folkestone, c. 1890* [Folkestone Central Library]

In 1882 a group of Anglican Evangelicals in Folkestone frustrated by their failure to put down 'high church' practices at most of the Anglican churches in the town, invited the Revd. N.R. Toke, rector of Knossington in Leicestershire, to begin a mission which would offer services based upon the Book of Common Prayer, but free from all 'high church' ceremonial and with strong

Evangelical teaching. The mission began by worshipping for a few weeks at Sandgate Wesleyan Methodist Church, at the invitation of that congregation, before it obtained temporary use of premises in Cheriton Road. The appeal for a permanent building was unsuccessful and was abandoned after the resignation of Toke in 1896, and the mission itself only survived until 1910. There were a number of other places where similar 'free' Church of England chapels were established, usually in opposition to a neighbouring ritualist church. Some were served by disillusioned Anglican clergymen, some by ministers of the Countess of Huntingdon's Connexion, and others formed part of either the Free Church of England or the Reformed Episcopal Church in England, two small denominations established by ex-Anglicans in the 1860's and 1870's.

'The Protestant Religion and Liberties of England I will maintain'. Motto on the Flag of the Prince of Orange, William III of England.

Emmanuel Mission Church (Church of England Unattached). Building in Temporary Occupation, Cheriton Road, Folkestone.

Protestant and Evangelical Services with Revised Liturgy.
Appeal for Erection of a Permanent Church.
Minister: Rev. N.R. Toke, M.A., (Late Rector of Knossington).

It has for a long time been felt by those who attend these Services that the fact of this Building being situated between a Brewery and a Coffee Tavern, has been detrimental to the success of the work which it is here sought to carry on; while experience has likewise shewn that the complete lack of anything approaching to Ecclesiastical Architecture in the external appearance of the place has prevented many visitors to the town from being able to find the Church.

These circumstances have led to the conclusion that an earnest effort ought at once to be made to secure a suitable site and obtain the necessary funds to erect a permanent Church building, and to this end therefore the Minister and Congregation invite the assistance of all who desire the maintenance and retention in England of those pure Evangelical principles of the Reformation in which our forefathers rejoiced.

That such a witness is urgently needed in Folkestone is clearly shewn by the fact, that out of the seven Church of England places of worship in the town, no less than five are Ritualistic, and only two Evangelical, and in both of these that old Protestant landmark, the black gown, has been discarded, and the surplice substituted as the garb of the Preacher.

Who then will help in this witness for the Truth of God, and protest against surrounding superstition and error, and for the maintenance of the Protestant Reformed Religion, by taking a Collecting Card, or in other ways obtaining donations?

Donations may be paid to the Account of Emmanuel Mission Church at the National Provincial Bank of England, Folkestone, or sent to General Swinhoe, 10 Westbourne Gardens, Folkestone, or to Rev. N.R. Toke, 8 Westbourne Gardens, Folkestone, from whom likewise Collecting Cards and copies of this Appeal may be obtained.

28. *Francis Murray's reflections on the services in Chislehurst parish church and their gradual transformation after his appointment to the rectory in 1846* [History of Chislehurst, London, 1899, pp. 91–5]

> These published reflections are an interesting statement from a clergyman who had spent more than a half a century developing his parish, liturgically and pastorally, in accordance with the ideas put forward initially in the *Tracts for the Times*. It should be noted that Murray, although an extreme 'high churchman', exercised considerable caution and restraint in making liturgical changes, though he still managed to alienate his more Evangelical parishioners, who petitioned successive archbishops of Canterbury against him and eventually established a new church free from Tractarian error.

With regard to the services in the parish church, it may be interesting to note the following state of things, as far as I am aware of them, before I became rector, and to state briefly some of the changes subsequently made.

The late rector, the Rev. Francis Dawson, was not much resident for the nine previous years; the Rev. Charles Caffin was curate, the Rev. Thomas Hussey occasionally assisting, and also the Rev. P. Welland. There was morning service on Sundays, with sermon, and afternoon service without sermon; this had been the practice for many years. There was not any service during the week, and the celebration of the Holy Communion took place only six times during the year. The amount of the offertory, being only collected at those times, was in the year before (May 1846) £14, and was devoted to the poor. No doubt there were some special collections occasionally at other times, but the above appears to have been the usual practice.

I believe that I at once began a monthly celebration, but I made no other change till service was instituted on St. Matthew's Day, 1846, in the morning and evening. I am not sure whether there was a celebration in the morning. I recollect that I at once began a sermon at the afternoon service on Sundays, as well as in the morning, and there were added services on Wednesday and Friday mornings.

As an indication of the strange state of feeling in the minds of some persons at that time, a lady coming from Sidcup, and hearing the bells ringing for evening service on a week day, asked why that was, and was told that "the new rector had begun a service on Saints' days". She wrote a letter to me afterwards, though not a parishioner, remonstrating with me, and saying that "she had not so learned Christ". These little incidents are useful as giving some idea of the state of mind of some persons then, caused by neglect of the offices of the Church and want of proper teaching in respect of the simple order of the Prayer Book.

In the following Lent I remember that then, for the first time, there was service morning and evening in Holy Week, 1847, with a sermon in the evening of each day on the Seven Words of our Lord. There were excellent congregations on those evenings. I think all remained much as this until 1848, when the alteration of the church was proposed.

During the alteration of the church in 1848–49 service was held in the room over part of the stables at Camden, by the kind permission of Mrs. Martin, then occupying the house. This was a very convenient substitute for the time; I remember that at that period there were only monthly celebrations, with the addition of those on Saints' days.

I do not recollect any special change of services at once after the reconsecration of the church in 1849. I think an evening service must have been then begun on Sundays. I remember coming to a resolution that I might begin a weekly celebration after Easter, or about that time, in 1850, but I cannot be certain when that was actually commenced.

In 1864 a definite advance was made according to the paper, which it is well to reprint here, as indicating the objects proposed and the principles upon which they were based. I am very thankful to say that since that Advent the services have been maintained according to the proposals of that paper:–

To the Parishioners of Chislehurst

In commencing with this Advent the more full and complete order of Daily Prayer in this Church, by the addition of the Service at 5, and a more perfect order of the Weekly Offertory, I wish to address a few words to you with the desire of commending these two observances to your devout attention.

I. OF DAILY PRAYER

If you will open the Prayer Book, just before the beginning of the Morning Service, you will see this plain general direction given as the rule to guide both priests and people in the use of that book: "The Order for Morning and Evening Prayer daily to be said and used throughout the year". And at the end of the Preface "concerning the Service of the Church" these words occur: "And all priests and deacons are to say daily the Morning and Evening Prayer, either privately or openly, not being let by sickness, or by some other urgent cause. And the curate (or clergyman) that ministereth in every Parish Church or Chapel, being at home, and not being otherwise reasonably hindered, shall say the same in the Parish Church or Chapel where he ministereth; and shall cause a bell to be tolled thereunto as convenient before he begin, that the people may come to hear God's Word and to pray with him".

This is the plain old rule of the Church of England establishing the principle of the Daily Worship of God in His Sanctuary, according to the command of the Lord, "My House shall be called the House of Prayer"; according to the interpretation put upon that command by the Apostles "St. Peter and St. John", who "went up together into the Temple at the hour of Prayer, being the ninth hour" (Acts iii. 1) — "they continued daily in the Temple" (Acts ii. 46) — according to the words of the Psalm, "Prayer shall be made ever unto Him, and daily shall He be praised" (Psalm lxxii. 15), and the noble words which are sung in the *Te Deum*, "Day by day we magnify Thee".

The great principles upon which this holy practice is based are these:–

1. God Almighty, though He appoints one-seventh portion of our time to be more specially given up to Him, yet nowhere restricts the Public Worship of His Name to one day, and there is no possible reason why we should do so.

2. As God provided, by the most express ordinance, for the daily sacrifice of the burnt-offering in the Jewish Temple, which formed the main, daily, unvarying worship of the Jews — so the Christian Church has always provided daily offices of public Service to be offered, to keep up the same principle of the continued offering from the people of Christ. The daily Morning and Evening Prayer is, in part, the fulfilment of this.

3. This alone provides for the adequate performance of the great duty of public intercession for the needs of the whole Church, and the peculiar wants of each parish.

4. As the family union of the household in prayer is the gathering into one the separately offered prayers of each individual, so likewise the united Daily Prayer in the Church is the gathering up before the Altar of the Parish Church of the worship of the various households. It will be seen from this that family prayer, though most necessary in itself, is no substitute, as is often thought, for the public Daily Worship of the Church.

Frequently this observation is made, as a test whether it is advisable to offer the Daily Service — How many persons attend it? As a matter of principle, this is not at all the question. Beyond all doubt, the greater the number, so much the better in every way; but in order to meet this thought as to the number of worshippers, our Lord especially gave His promise even to "two or three gathered together in His Name". But, in real truth, the great duty is independent of this — the duty of public daily intercession of priest and people in the House of Prayer, and the duty of simple, unhesitating obedience to the rule of the Church, founded upon the Word of God, which provides for this.

The hours of Daily Prayer will be:– Monday, Tuesday, Thursday, Saturday, 9.15 A.M.; Wednesday and Friday, 11 A.M., 7.30 P.M.

I hope that many persons will endeavour to order their time so as to admit of their joining in such acts of Daily Worship, as a part of the sacrifice due from them to God. Let each consider this in the light of a duty and a privilege, if the opportunity is offered, and other necessary engagements of life admit of it. If the duty be recognised, time will often be found; and time so given up will be found to sanctify and give a peace and order to many other hours of occupation.

II. THE WEEKLY OFFERTORY.

About two years since I brought this subject before you in two sermons. I showed then how the alms offered before God in this Church had increased from £14 in 1840 (the earliest record which I have) to £368 in 1862 and £492 in 1863; forming a general amount, from the year 1846 to 1863, of £4200; and this exclusive of general parish subscriptions, the money expended on the Church, and other private charity.

I do not bring this before you now to parade such a fact, but in thankfulness before God for the abundant fruit shown by you in this way, and to suggest this special thought; if the prayers and alms of Cornelius "went up as a memorial before God", may we not humbly trust that these alms here offered have gone up as a like "memorial" before the Eternal Throne for many souls in this place, as some part of "a good foundation against the time to come"? (Tim. vi.). "God is not unrighteous that He will forget your works and labour that proceedeth of love" (Heb. vi.).

My dear Brethren, shall we not proceed in such a good work? I think that the time has come when we should do this in a more regular and systematic manner, not only when the Holy Eucharist is celebrated, but each Sunday and Holy Day.

The almsgiving of Christians should be based on these principles:–

1. The great duty of endeavouring to devote to the service of God a

tenth portion, if possible, of the means with which He has blessed them, underlies all that God has taught His people from the beginning; we see this in Genesis xiv. 20. This duty was taken up and fully enforced under the Levitical Law, and has passed on unchanged and undiminished into the Christian. It has formed from the beginning, and still continues, one of the primary laws of God in respect of the offerings of His people.

2. St. Paul (I Cor. xvi. 2) teaches the principle of a weekly setting apart of some offering to God — "Upon the first day of the week let every one of you lay by him store as God hath prospered him". Here is inculcated upon all the time of the dedication of their offering and the measure of the offering.

If these duties be once acknowledged and understood, then most persons will be thankful to find in the Church a means both of offering and of sanctifying their gifts.

We would desire to give this opportunity for the voluntary offerings of each person through the weekly offertory; there is no obligation implied in presenting that opportunity; it will be left to the conscience and desire of each individual member of the congregation. We only fulfil our duty in giving the opportunity according to the law of the Church, which we, on our part, have simply no right to set aside.

In complying with this, we are but acting upon what various members of the congregation have at different times pressed upon us.

With regard to all offerings thus made, it should be remembered that each person is fully at liberty to dedicate their offering in any manner they desire, by enclosing it in paper and stating the object; and that, as our Blessed Lord tells us, it is "the altar that sanctifieth the gift" (Matt. xxiii. 19).

It is not, in any way, implied that all the "charity" of Christian persons should, or ought to, pass through the offertory. This is left to the discretion and the wish of each person.

I repeat that we have no right to withhold the opportunity of the weekly offertory from those who may desire to offer of their substance weekly to God in Church, and to sanctify that by offering it upon His altar.

Upon the first and third Sundays of the month, and upon all days when there is a celebration of the Holy Communion, the offertory will be as usual during that service, a pause being left at the end of the prayer for the Church Militant for any persons to leave the Church, if they desire it. There is no necessity for any to leave, even though they do not communicate; The Church does not require them to leave, and any persons who wish to remain as an act of devotion, are fully permitted to do so.

Upon the other Sundays when there is no second celebration, after the offertory and the prayer for the Church Militant the service will end with one of the Collects and the Benediction.

It is hoped so to order the Service that there will be scarcely any additional length. Some persons will gain a privilege which I doubt not many among you will value; and we shall all profit by not losing that most beautiful and comprehensive prayer "for the whole state of Christ's Church Militant here on earth".

It is proposed to devote the Offertory as follows:–

On the first Sunday of the month, and on all the greater Festivals, to the poor.

On the second Sunday of the month, to the Clergy.

On the third Sunday of the month, to the Church Fund — providing sundry things required for the care and services of the Church.

On the fourth Sunday of the month, to the expenses of the Organ and Choir.

On the fifth Sunday of the month, to Missions.

The Offertory at all the early celebrations, except on the first Sunday of the month and the greater Festivals, will be devoted as now to the Church Fund.

Commending you to the love of Almighty God,
I am your affectionate Friend and Pastor,
FRANCIS H. MURRAY, Rector.

Week before Advent, 1864

It was in the year 1871, after I had been at the "Passion Play" at Ober-Ammergau, that, being alone on a Sunday at the then small village of St. Ulrich, the head place of sacred, and also of ordinary, wood-carving in the Austrian Tyrol, and after reading some work of Dr. Neale, I was guided to the thought that the offering of the daily Eucharist should be and might be resumed at St. Nicholas and at the Church of the Annunciation. On returning home, I preached four sermons on the subject, bringing it clearly and definitely before the congregation. I did not at once propose to commence such an important change, but I asked them to make it the subject of prayer for guidance, and, if that was given, I suggested that the offering should commence at the following Easter. That was done by the grace of God, and has been continued ever since.

29. *Complaints about ritualist innovations at Aylesford in 1900* [KAO, P12/8/1]

These complaints were made at the annual vestry meeting held on 16 April 1900. Aylesford was at that time one of about forty

Anglican churches in Kent in which the eucharistic vestments were in use, part of the significant changes introduced by the Revd. G.B. Vaux, vicar from 1896 until 1902. The dissatisfaction expressed in 1900 had been foreshadowed in the previous year when the vestry had opposed the re-election of one of the church-wardens, who had Vaux's support, though he was re-elected by 219 votes to 132 after a poll of the parish had been demanded.

Mr. Walmsley said that the parishioners had complained of the way in which the services had been conducted by the vicar and he wished it to be recorded in the minutes that the Inhabitants objected to his teaching and he hoped the Vicar would have a meeting of the Inhabitants to discuss the various matters in connection with the Church service. He complained of wafer bread being used at the Communion and said he could not partake of the Sacrament because he was not in Love and Charity with the Vicar.

Mr. G.L. Hawkes objected to the Altar Book being used by the children.

Mr. Leegood objected to the use of candles on the Altar.

After others had spoken the Vicar said with reference to the Altar Book of which complaint had been made, and which some one had sent a copy to the Lord Bishop of Rochester,* the Bishop had returned the copy with the remark that he entirely agreed with the information contained therein and he thought it a most useful book.

With reference to the bread used at Holy Communion he said wafer bread had never been used by him and he did not intend using it.

Mr. Walmsley apologised and the meeting ended.

30. *Copy of the draft constitution of the Benedictine community of nuns at Malling Abbey submitted to Archbishop Frederick Temple in 1901* [Lambeth Palace Library, Temple Papers, vol. 47, ff. 39–40]

The Anglican Benedictine community at Malling Abbey had been founded by the eccentric Fr. Ignatius (the Revd. J.L. Lyne) at Feltham in 1868. In 1879, however, there was a schism in the community the majority of which was 'excommunicated' by its founder. It was these 'excommunicated' nuns who moved to Malling Abbey in 1893 after the property had been purchased by Miss Charlotte Boyd and vested in what was known as 'The English Abbey Restoration Trust'. Subsequent developments did

---

* Edward Stuart Talbot (1844–1934), himself a 'high churchman'. Talbot was first warden of Keble College, Oxford, 1870–89; vicar of Leeds, 1889–95; bishop of Rochester, 1895–1905, Southwark, 1905–11 and Winchester 1911–23.

not augur well for the community. Miss Boyd and two chaplains in succession became Roman Catholics, Miss Boyd purchasing the Slipper Chapel at Walsingham which later became the Roman Catholic shrine. The secessions provoked considerable 'strife, discord and decay of discipline' in the community (Temple Papers, vol. 25, ff. 60–3; vol. 47, ff. 1–6) until the election of a new abbess in 1907. By 1911 the community had become too large for Malling Abbey and moved to Milford Haven, where in 1913 the majority of the nuns decided, with the neighbouring Anglican Benedictine monks at Caldey, to submit to the Roman claims. The present successor of the original Anglican community at Malling Abbey is the Roman Catholic one established at Talacre in North Wales since 1920.

The present Anglican community at Malling Abbey, also of Benedictine nuns, began as the Community of The Holy Redeemer at Edmonton in 1891 and moved to Malling Abbey at the invitation of the English Abbey Restoration Trust in 1916. For the history of both Anglican communities at Malling Abbey see P.F. Anson, *The Call of the Cloister*, rev. ed. London, 1964, pp. 418–28, 462–6.

Name
The Congregation of S.S. Mary and Scholastica

The Congregation of S.S. Mary and Scholastica is a Community of Women living under the Rule of St. Benedict in accordance with the traditional interpretation of the Above Institute.

The Superior

The Superior is elected for life by a three fourths majority of the Professed.

The Superior has the absolute appointment of all Conventual Offices (for example Prioress, Novice Mistress, etc.).

Miss Harriet Emily Stewart has been appointed for life by a unanimous vote of the Chapter. The Chapter consists of the Mother Superior, and the Professed Choir Sisters.

Each Choir Sister enters the Chapter a year from the day of her Profession.

The Chapter are to be called together for the Election of Superior — Novices — Professed — and the expulsion of any Professed Sister.

The Chapter by a unanimous vote can depose the Superior for evil living, and for wasting the revenue of the Congregation.

The Chapter must be consulted before any large undertaking is commenced, for minor matters it is sufficient for the Superior to consult two or three of the discreet ones. In Chapter the Mother Superior always has a casting vote.

The Divine Office

The following Offices are to be said or sung, as they are found in the Monastic Breviary either in English or Latin. And the Obligation shall be considered fulfilled if the Ferial Office is said.

The Divine Offices

Matins.	Terce.	Vespers &
Lauds.	Sext.	Compline.
Prime.	Nones.	

The Divine Offices must be said everyday throughout the year, and may only be omitted on account of Plague — fire — the Queen's Enemies, or the Act of God.

No Office shall be omitted on any pretext whatever, if only one Sister can be present, she is still to say the Office aloud, as being a public Act for the Community, unless hindered by circumstances over which she has no control.

Here let it be noted that in times of grievous sickness it is sufficient at Matins only to say appointed Psalms. Offices are not as a rule to be said by accumulation, but the Superior has power to order this on special occasions.

The Chaplain

The Chaplain is appointed by the Mother Superior. He must be a Priest of seven years standing, or thirty-five years of age.

He can be called upon by the Superior to resign for heresy, or evil living; in which case there is to be an appeal to the Bishop whose decision shall be final.

The Chaplain has a right to be at the deliberative Chapters, and speak, but has no vote.

The Property

No Sister, whether dismissed or not, whether remaining or not, or her heirs, executors, or administrators, shall have or be entitled, either in her lifetime or after her decease, to, or shall have power to claim, either at law or in Equity any estate, right, title, interest, property, or share whatsoever in or to the real estate or chattels, real houses, leasehold or copyhold estates sticks, funds, and monies, or in, or to the household furniture, books, linen, china, and other chattels personal and effects belonging to, or held in trust for, or used for the purposes of the said Congregation, or any of them or any part or parts thereof, anything herein contained to the contrary thereof in any wise notwithstanding.

Note Before a Postulant can be clothed (i.e. made a novice) or a novice professed, she must procure the consent of the Superior to be put up for Election.

Work

No work must be undertaken incompatible with saying the Divine Office.

Works recommended. Educational. Boarders, care of Aged and sick. Penitentiary work is forbidden and any work which would oblige the Sisters to leave the house or grounds.

Appeal to the Bishop

In case of a difference of opinion between the whole of the Chapter, and the Superior, there shall be first of all an appeal to the Chaplain when if either is not ready to accept his decision there shall be a further appeal to the Bishop of the diocese (if he be willing to act) whose decision shall be final.

31. *Deed of Trust to prevent the dispersal or destruction of vestments at Folkestone parish church, 22 June 1904* [Folkestone Parish Archives]

Many 'high church' clergymen were concerned that present or future ecclesiastical legislation could be used by the bishops to deprive a parish of illegal ornaments or vestments and were anxious to devise ways in which these might be protected. In some parishes they were considered to be the personal property of the incumbent (and in some they actually were). The setting up of a vestment trust, as at Folkestone, was another method devised to circumvent episcopal authority and was copied in other parts of the country to protect likely targets of Protestant attack, as at Walsingham, where the shrine of Our Lady established by the incumbent in 1931 was vested in a college of guardians outside the jurisdiction of the diocesan bishop.

This indenture made the twenty second day of June, One thousand nine hundred and four, Between the Reverend Erskine William Knollys, M.A., the vicar of the Parish Church of Folkestone in the County of Kent known as 'St. Mary and St. Eanswythe' of the one part, and Edward William Hansell of 93 Gloucester Place, Portman Square in the County of London, Barrister-at-Law, John Edgar Calveley

Hordern, manager of Branch of the 'Union of London and Smiths' Bank Limited' at Canterbury in the County of Kent, and Henry Albert Powell of 44 Sandgate Road, Folkestone aforesaid, surgeon, of the other part. Whereas the several Eucharistic or other vestments specified in the Schedule hereunder written have been delivered over by the said Erskine William Knollys to the said Edward William Hansell, John Edgar Calveley Hordern and Henry Albert Powell with the intent that the same shall be held by them upon the trusts and subject to the provisions hereinafter declared and contained. Now it is hereby agreed and declared as follows:

1. The said Edward William Hansell, John Edgar Calveley Hordern and Henry Albert Powell . . . shall henceforth . . . stand possessed of the said vestments upon trust that the said trustees shall permit the said Erskine William Knollys . . . and other the Vicar for the time being thereof and any assisting clergy . . . to wear and use the same in the celebration of the services in the said Parish Church and shall for the purposes of such use permit the said Erskine William Knollys and other the Vicar for the time being using the said vestments to keep the same in and under his sole custody and control.

2. The Vicar for the time being of the said Parish Church . . . shall during such time as he shall have the custody of the said vestments at his own expense keep the same insured against loss or damage by fire and burglary. . . .

3. The said Trustees shall at the termination of the period aforesaid* stand possessed of the said vestments upon trust for the person who shall then be the Vicar of the said Parish Church . . . . . the said Erskine William Knollys hereby expressing an earnest hope that such Vicar. . . . . . will declare similar trusts of the said vestments.

4. Provided that notwithstanding anything herein contained if any of the following events shall happen, that is to say if the Vicar for the time being shall (a) in anywise alter any of the said vestments or (b) omit to keep on foot either of the said insurances or (c) for any reason whatever discontinue the use of the said vestments or any of them in the celebration of the services of the said Parish Church, such Vicar shall thereupon if the said Trustees shall require him so to do deliver back all the said vestments to the said Trustees who shall have power to retake possession of the same and to retain the same in their custody for so long as they shall

* Twenty one years after the death of the last surviving descendant of Queen Victoria living in 1904.

think fit during the continuance in his office of the Vicar so deprived of the use and custody thereof.

5. The said Trustees or a majority of them shall have absolute power to determine any question or doubt which may arise as to whether any of the aforesaid events has happened so as to entitle the said Trustees to retake possession of the said vestments and such determination shall be conclusive.

6. And it is hereby declared that the power of appointing new Trustees conferred by the Trustee Act 1893 Section 10 shall apply to these presents and to the trusts hereby created.

The Schedule above referred to:

White Festal Chasuble of cream gothic damask, Y cross of green gothic damask with design of vine leaves and grapes embroidered on it, embroidered 'Agnus' in centre of Y cross at the back, cross edged with 3/8" green and gold lace, blue daisy lining. Stole, Maniple and apparel for Amice to match.

Yellow and white Simpler Festal Chasuble of yellow and white Japanese damask, Y cross of blue and gold brocatelle edged with ¼" blue and gold lace, plain blue lining. Stole and Maniple to match.

Red chasuble of red gothic damask design on Y cross in gold outline with bands of red and gold lace dividing sections, Cross of red velvet, Shield in centre with raised gold sacred monogram. Stole, Maniple and apparel for Amice to match.

Blue Lenten Chasuble of blue gothic damask Y cross of red silk velvet edged with 3/8" red and gold lace, lined with red Chinois lining design on Y cross gold I.H.C.'s and M.'s alternating paned up with red and gold lace, shield in centre with thorn wreath and nails. Stole, Maniple and apparel for Amice to match.

Chasuble of black Japanese damask Y cross formed by 2½" black and gold lace edged with 2 rows of black and gold cord, Shield in centre of cross with raised gold monogram, lining blue chinois. Stole, Maniple and apparel for Amice to match.

Green Chasuble of green gothic damask, Y cross of blue and gold brocatelle, sacred monogram on back, old gold lining. Stole, Maniple and apparel for Amice to match.

Cope: Festal Cope of red and gold brocatelle, Orphrey of red gothic damask with monograms in raised gold, Hood with medallion of Madonna and Child, morse damask embroidered with gold and set with nine Topazes.

Vestment Chest of teak and oak wood.

Cope Chest of oak lined with tin.

32. *Extracts from the Minutes of Evidence published by the Royal Commission on Ecclesiastical Discipline in 1906* [Rochester Cathedral Library]

The Royal Commission on Ecclesiastical Discipline was set up in 1904, as a result of continued Evangelical agitation against ritualism, and reported two years later, recommending in favour of some relaxation of permitted liturgical practices to accommodate moderate 'high churchmen', but against those innovations which it regarded as being totally inconsistent with traditional Anglican doctrine and practice since the Reformation. The commission heard detailed evidence, mostly given by Evangelical witnesses, on the celebration of 687 services in 559 churches throughout England and Wales, including a small number in Kent. The evidence for four such services is printed here: a solemn celebration of Holy Communion with incense at St. Saviour's, Folkestone; a more old-fashioned celebration of Mattins and Holy Communion, as well as an early celebration of the latter, at St. Mary's, Strood; and a simple weekday celebration of Holy Communion at St. Barnabas', Tunbridge Wells.

[Minute 341: St. Saviour's, Folkestone; date of visit, Easter Sunday, 3 April 1904]

The service attended was the high celebration with sermon at 10.30. The congregation consisted very largely of children. Apart from the teachers in charge of the children there were not more than sixty adults present, while there must have been from 200 to 300 children, some of whom were very young. There are two altars in the church, one in the chancel and a smaller one on the south side of the chancel. On the retable of the altar in the chancel there were six candles, all of them being lighted for the celebration. Over this altar is a canopy. A wooden screen divides the chancel from the body of the church, and on the top of the screen there is a large framed picture of the Crucifixion. There is another picture of the Crucifixion over the altar in the chancel. The following points were noted during the celebration: Mass vestments were worn, the celebrant being vested in a cream silk chasuble. He was attended by two boys vested in scarlet cassocks, albs and red girdles who acted as servers. The celebrant appeared to make his confession at the altar steps, and on reaching the altar bent down and appeared to kiss it. Before reading the Gospel, the celebrant made the sign of the Cross on the Gospel Book and on his forehead, lips, and breast; and at the conclusion he kissed the Gospel Book. The chalice was mixed in view of the congregation. After the elements had been placed on the altar the thurifer brought the censer and the celebrant censed the elements and then the altar. The celebrant performed the *Lavabo*. During the singing of the *Sanctus* the celebrant appeared to engage in some secret ceremony over the elements, making the sign of the Cross over them. During the Prayer of Consecration incense was burnt. The manual acts were hidden. After the consecration of the bread the celebrant genuflected before it, and elevated a wafer above his head, again genuflecting. The same procedure followed in connection with the chalice after the consecration of the wine. After the Prayer of Consecration the celebrant again engaged in secret devotions and frequently genuflected. There was only one communicant.

[Minute 5269: St. Barnabas', Tunbridge Wells; date of visit, Whit Monday, 23 May 1904]

The ornaments and fittings were: two Communion Tables, one in the chancel, with a cross and six candles above it, and one in the chapel on the south side of the chancel, with a cross and two candles (lighted) above it; a structure resembling a tabernacle, just above the Holy Table in the chapel, with a red lamp burning before it; seven red lamps suspended before the Holy Table in the chancel, six banners in the chancel, and two in the chapel, and a crucifix above the chancel screen, with figures of, presumably, St. Mary and St. John. There were the folllowing notices: one, headed 'Confessions', stating the times at which confessions are heard, in all seven times each week, and another headed 'Brethren, pray for us', giving the names of sick, recovered, and departed persons. The service I attended was Holy Communion, at 8 a.m. It was held in the chapel. Three altar cards were on the Holy Table. The celebrant, who was attended by a server, wore a dark red chasuble, an alb, and a stole. The Ten Commandments and the Prayer for the King were omitted. At the reading of the Gospel, the celebrant made the sign of the Cross upon his forehead, his lips and his breast. He mixed the chalice during the service. He performed the *Lavabo*. He made the sign of the Cross in the air when pronouncing the Absolution. During the Prayer of Consecration he concealed the manual acts by bending his body over the elements. After pronouncing the words of consecration he genuflected before the elements. He elevated the paten and the chalice to the level of his forehead, and genuflected at the close of the prayer. During the prayer the server knelt, with his head on the ground. After the prayer there was a long pause, during which the celebrant was apparently engaged in secret prayers and ceremonies, genuflecting several times before the elements. The celebrant then turned round to the congregation, and holding up a wafer said, 'Behold The Lamb of God which taketh away the sin of the world'. There were about fifteen communicants, but there were quite as many who did not communicate. At the close of the Prayer Book service, the celebrant went to the north-west corner of the Holy Table and read secretly, genuflecting towards the end. This is in accordance with the practice of reading the Last Gospel in the Roman Missal.

[Minute: 12481: St. Mary's, Strood; date of visit, 30 October 1904]

The services I attended were, Holy Communion at 8 a.m. and 11 a.m. (choral), and Morning Prayer at 10.30 a.m. Among the ornaments in the church I found the following: a brass cross and fourteen candles on or above the Holy Table, and two candles on the floor on either side of the Holy Table, a processional cross and two banners in the chancel, and a crucifix by the pulpit. The early celebration was announced for 8 a.m. but the service began about thirteen minutes later. The celebrant was vested in amice, alb, girdle, stole, chasuble and maniple. Two candles were lighted on or above the Holy Table. A lad vested in scarlet cassock and lace-trimmed cotta, who entered the chancel at 8.27 acted as server during the latter part of the service. The Prayer for the King was omitted. The clergyman knelt at the *Incarnatus* in the Creed, and crossed himself at the end at the words "and the life of the world to come". He also made the sign of the Cross towards the people when pronouncing the Absolution and the Blessing, and frequently over the elements before and after consecration. The chalice was ceremonially mixed during the service. After the words of consecration were pronounced, the clergyman genuflected to, and then elevated, the wafer, a ceremony which was repeated with the chalice. The turret bell was rung three times at each elevation. When administering the Communion the clergyman made the sign of the Cross with the wafer and the chalice before each communicant. Morning Prayer began a few minutes after 10.30, there being neither choir nor music. The opening Exhortation was omitted, as were the General Thanksgiving, and the Prayers for All Sorts and Conditions of Men, for the Royal Family and for the Bishops and Clergy. The *Venite* was also omitted. During the concluding part of Morning Prayer the church bells were rung, and when this service was over a server lighted sixteen candles on or above the Holy Table. Shortly after 11 a procession, consisting of seven choir boys, a crucifer, bearing a processional crucifix, a banner-bearer with banner, a server, and the celebrant vested in a cope, entered the chancel. Incense was then brought in, and having been blessed, the Holy Table was censed. The celebrant then said, "Let us go forth in peace", and the procession, accompanied by a lad swinging the censer, moved twice round the church, while a hymn was being sung. On returning to the Holy Table, the clergyman took off his cope and appeared vested in amice, alb, girdle, stole, chasuble, and maniple. An introit was then sung, and at nearly 11.20 the service as in the Book of Common Prayer was commenced. A hymn was sung after the Epistle, though the words could not be distinguished. The clergyman knelt at the *Incarnatus* in the Creed, and crossed himself at the words, "and the life of the world to come". The clergyman removed his chasuble before preaching the sermon, resuming it again on his return to the Holy Table. The *Benedictus Qui Venit* was sung immediately before the Prayer of Consecration. During the Prayer of Consecration the manual acts were not visible. After the words of consecration the clergyman knelt for some few moments, elevated the wafer, and again genuflected. This ceremony was repeated at the consecration of the wine. The turret bell was rung three times after each elevation. After the Prayer of Consecration, the *Agnus Dei* and a hymn were sung. The clergyman made the sign of the Cross with each element when administering the Communion to each individual communicant, also towards the people when pronouncing the Blessing.

NOTES ON ILLUSTRATIONS

1. Seating plan of Chiddingstone Church, 1724 [KAO, P89/7/1]

   This illustration shows the liturgical arrangements typical in most Anglican churches in the eighteenth and early nineteenth centuries. The numbers on the pews indicate the properties to which these seats were appropriated. Nos. 3–5 mark the pulpit, reading-pew and clerk's seat. Note also the absence of pews around the altar permitting the communicants to draw near on Sacrament Sundays.

2. John Whichcord's vision of All Saints, Maidstone, in *c.* 1400 [KAO, Office Library]

   The younger Whichcord (1823–85) was a Maidstone-based architect who published a scholarly study of the town's, formerly collegiate, parish church in 1845. This illustration shows the rather inaccurate and romantic understanding of the Middle Ages common in the mid-nineteenth century, but it was this highly idealised picture which was the model on which most church architects after 1840 based their designs for new and restored churches.

3. Interior of Christ Church, Kilndown, as refitted in 1840–5 [Council for the Care of Churches]

   This church was the earliest one in Kent to be refitted according to the ideals of the Cambridge Camden Society, and still retains virtually all the decoration and furnishings shown in this illustration.

4. Interior of East Farleigh Church as restored in 1891 [Kent County Library, Local History Collection]

   Although East Farleigh was connected with the Oxford Movement during the respective incumbencies of Robert and Henry Wilberforce before 1850, this restoration of the church by J.L. Pearson was not carried out until 1891. It is a typical example of the sensitive restorations carried out by 'high church' architects like Pearson by the last quarter of the nineteenth century.

5. Frontispiece from the *Directorium Anglicanum*, published in 1858,

which showed 'high church' clergyman how the liturgy of the Church of England could be carried out according to the type of ceremonial familiar in English churches before the Reformation. The illustration shows the solemn celebration of the Holy Eucharist with celebrant, deacon and sub-deacon properly vested in chasuble, dalmatic and tunicle, and the type of sanctuary furnishings approved of by the ritualist clergy at the time.

6 and 7. Bodley's drawings of Bicknor church as it was before restoration in 1858 and as it was to appear after the restoration programme had been completed [KAO, U449 P6]

These delightful drawings, signed by Bodley, show a typical Kentish church before restoration, with three-decker pulpit and high box-pews. Note how Bodley's plans for the restoration shift the emphasis from the pulpit to the altar, create a much greater sense of spaciousness in the building, and greatly increase its height by the removal of the plaster ceiling.

8 and 9. Kemsing church before restoration in 1870 and after re-fitting by Comper in 1902 [Council for the Care of Churches]

These illustrations show a similar contrast to that in the Bodley drawings. At Kemsing, however, the transformation was achieved more gradually than at Bicknor, and Comper has been much more effective in recreating a good deal of the likely atmosphere of a medieval village church.

10. Drawing of the new organ case in Rochester Cathedral, 1876 [KAO, Office Library]

This illustration shows the very fine organ case designed by Sir G.G. Scott as part of his major restoration of Rochester Cathedral in the 1870's. The fine workmanship of the case is now much less obvious, as shortly afterwards the plain choir screen was faced with a series of statues and the flight of steps to the choir considerably reduced by an alteration in the floor levels.

11. Canon Matthew Woodward, vicar of Folkestone 1851–98 [Folkestone Central Library]

This photograph was taken in 1892 and shows Woodward in surplice and coloured stole, the latter being still in use at Folkestone parish church, and carrying a biretta, a form of head-covering much favoured by the ritualist clergy as a symbol of priestly authority.

12. Details from the Stations of the Cross in Folkestone parish church, *c.* 1900 [Folkestone Parish Church]

These four pictures are part of an elaborate scheme of illustration devised by Matthew Woodward for the walls of his parish church, much of which still survives. Stations of the Cross are still only to be found in very definitely Anglo-Catholic churches, and those at Folkestone are among the earliest surviving ones anywhere in England.

13. Sanctuary of Folkestone parish church as refitted in 1885 [Folkestone Central Library]

This is a typical 'high church' sanctuary of the period. Note the elaborate stencilling on the walls, the marble reredos and sanctuary panelling, the handsome altar frontal and the altar ornaments.

14. Interior of East Malling church, *c.* 1900 [Kent County Library, Local History Collection]

This illustration shows the treatment of a village church in a similar manner to the works carried out at Folkestone parish church. At East Malling there are painted scenes over the chancel arch and the nave walls, and the roof has also been painted with appropriate scriptural texts.

15 and 16. Interiors of St. Barnabas, Tunbridge Wells, and Holy Trinity, Broadstairs, *c.* 1900 [Kent County Library, Local History Collection]

These two illustrations show two contrasting Anglo-Catholic interiors at the turn of the century. One shows the typical grandeur of some churches specifically designed for Anglo-Catholic worship (Tunbridge Wells), and the other the typical clutter that tended to be created when buildings designed primarily for preaching had to be adapted to the requirements of a more elaborate ritual (Broadstairs).

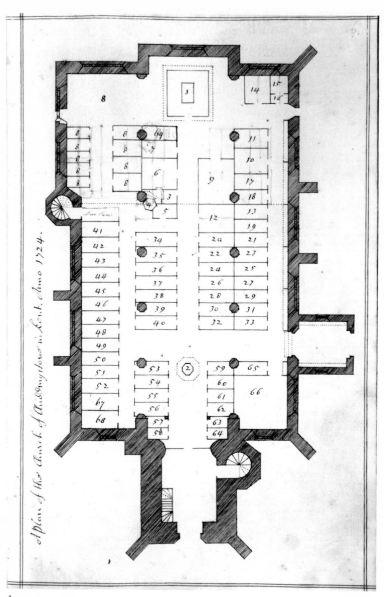

1.

2.

3.

4.

5.

S. James. Bicknor. Kent. 1858.

6.

7.

127

8.

9.

ORGAN CASE: ROCHESTER CATHEDRAL.——The late Sir G. G. Scott, Architect.

10.

11.

12a.

12b.

12c.

12d.

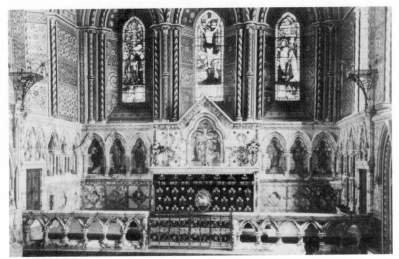

13.

14.

15.

16.

GLOSSARY OF TERMS

alb   a tunic of white cloth, reaching to the feet and enveloping the entire person, worn by clerics.

amice   a hood of white cloth, worn by clerics.

aumbry   a cupboard, locker or closed recess in the church wall for books, sacramental vessels, vestments, etc., or for keeping the reserved sacrament in, see *tabernacle*

biretta   a square raised cap worn by Roman Catholic, and some Anglican, clerics.

broach   a spire carried up on four of its sides from the top of a square tower.

burse   a receptacle for the corporal or linen cloth used to cover the elements in the eucharist.

cassock   a long close-fitting tunic worn by clerics, vergers, choristers and others engaged in ecclesiastical functions.

chalice   a cup in which the wine is consecrated and administered in the celebration of the eucharist.

chantry   a chapel, altar or part of a church endowed for the maintenance of one or more priests to say mass for the souls of the founders or others specified by them.

chasuble   a coloured or plain linen vestment worn by the priest over the alb *(q.v.)* in the celebration of the eucharist.

corona   a circular chandelier either suspended from the roof of a church or supported on a stand.

cotta   a shortened form of surplice *(q.v.)*.

credence   a small table or shelf on which the eucharistic elements are placed previous to consecration.

crucifer   a person who carries a cross in an ecclesiastical procession.

crucifix   an image or figure of Christ upon the cross.

dalmatic   an ecclesiastical vestment with wide sleeves worn over the alb *(q.v.)* by deacons at the celebration of the eucharist and on other occasions.

135

dossal	an ornamental cloth hung at the back of the altar or at the sides of the chancel.
faldstool	a small desk at which the Litany is appointed to be said or sung.
frontal	a movable covering for the front of an altar, generally of embroidered cloth or silk.
groin	architectural term denoting edge formed by the intersection of two vaults, or the rib of stone or wood with which this is usually covered.
hassock	a cushion for kneeling on.
jamb	side post of a doorway or window.
lancet	a tall narrow window
lavabo	the ritual washing of the priest's hands at the offertory in the celebration of the eucharist.
maniple	a narrow strip of material worn suspended from the left arm near the wrist by the priest, deacon and subdeacon during the celebration of the eucharist.
missal	a book containing the order of service for the celebration of the eucharist.
monial	alternative name for a mullion *(q.v.)*
mullion	a vertical bar dividing the sections of a screen or window.
orphrey	an ornamental border or band on an ecclesiastical vestment.
paten	a circular plate or shallow dish on which the bread is laid at the celebration of the eucharist.
piscina	a perforated stone basin set into the wall on the south side of the altar, for carrying away the water used for rinsing the chalice after the celebration.
pyx	vessel in which the consecrated bread of the eucharist is reserved, see *aumbry* and *tabernacle*.
quatrefoil	architectural term denoting a sculpture in the form of four radiating leaves or petals.
reredos	an ornamental screen of stone or wood covering the wall at the back of an altar.
retable	a shelf or ledge raised above the back of an altar on which ornaments may be placed.
sacrarium	that part of a church immediately surrounding the altar,

also called the sanctuary.

sconce   an ornamental bracket for holding one or more candles.

sedilia   a series of seats, usually three in number, placed on the south side of the altar for the use of the clergy.

spandrel   architectural term devoting the triangular space between the outer curve of an arch and the rectangle formed by the mouldings enclosing it, or the space between the shoulders of two contiguous arches and the mouldings above them.

superfrontal   a covering of embroidered cloth or silk hanging over the upper edge of an altar frontal *(q.v.)*.

surplice   a loose vestment of white linen worn over the cassock *(q.v.)* by clerics, choristers and others taking part in church services.

tabernacle   an ornamented receptacle for the pyx *(q.v.)* placed on or above the altar for the reservation of the sacrament, see *aumbry*.

thurifer   a person who carries the censer or thurible for burning incense in religious ceremonies

tunicle   a vestment resembling the dalmatic *(q.v.)* worn by sub-deacons at the celebration of the eucharist.

INDEX OF PERSONS

INDEX OF PLACES